MW01611830

THE
LORD
and the landscaper

THE
LORD
and the landscaper
stories to challenge your walk with God

John Gordon

TATE PUBLISHING *& Enterprises*

TATE PUBLISHING
& Enterprises

The Lord and the Landscaper
Copyright © 2007 by John Gordon. All rights reserved.

Book design copyright © 2007 by Tate Publishing, LLC. All rights reserved.
Cover design by Janae Glass
Interior design by Taylor Rauschkolb
Published in the United States of America

ISBN: 978-1-5988674-3-5
07.03.22

This is what the Lord says:

"Let not the wise man boast of his wisdom
or the strong man boast of his strength
or the rich man boast of his riches,
but let him who boasts boast about this:
that he understands and knows me,
that I am the Lord, who exercises kindness,
justice and righteousness on earth,
for in these I delight," declares the Lord.

Jeremiah 9:23–24 (NIV)

Dedication

To Jesus, who has been my best friend for so many years now.

To my wife, Brenda (my Redhead), who has been a true companion since we were 18 years old.

To Frank Langston, my mentor, who resides in Heaven now.

To my children, Christopher and Jennifer, who I diligently pray will receive a double portion of the grace God has given me.

Acknowledgements

Thanks to Lori Hodge, who did some of the initial work for this book even when things weren't going so well in her life.

Special thanks to my spiritual daughter and editor, Stefanie Reubell, who labored diligently so we could get this book to print.

Thanks to my friends and acquaintances who read *The Lord and the Landscaper.* I appreciate your insight and encouragement.

Contents

11	Introduction
13	1. Hey, Mister
16	2. The Man in Blue Jeans and the Newly-Elected Congressman
19	3. The Glory
22	4. The Vision
25	5. The Beginning of a Prayer Life
28	6. The Accident that Was No Accident
31	7. My Scariest Moment with God
33	8. God's Friend
35	9. Five Days in Arkansas
38	10. Gypsy Rose Lee
40	11. A Day in Toronto
42	12. Senior English Class
44	13. Angry with God
47	14. Frank
50	15. Inconvenienced
53	16. The Greatest Miracle I Have Ever Seen
56	17. Aslan
59	18. Lassie
61	19. My Greatest Week of Prayer
65	20. A Girl Named Dalexia
69	21. Does God Heal?
71	22. AIDS and Brother Bill
75	23. The Con Man
78	24. Not Today
80	25. Go Buy Stamps
84	26. A Fast from Good Works
87	27. Flowers for a Girl
90	28. A Great Grandpa
93	29. Be a Servant

95	30. A Lesson from the World's Oldest Profession
98	31. Under the Bridge
101	32. A Church Destroyed
103	33. January 3, 1980
107	34. Tear It Up
109	35. A Friend
111	36. Krispy Kremes
115	37. Beauty
118	38. Pray for a Hero
121	39. Nobody
123	40. No More Babies
125	41. Little Things
128	42. The Defense Attorney
131	43. The Gladiator
134	44. The Washer and Dryer
136	45. Go by Bair's Grocery
138	46. Humiliated
140	47. The Angry Jew
143	48. Chicken and Catfish
145	49. Any Minute
149	50. Trust Me
152	51. Heart Surgery and Beyond
155	52. Your Story

Introduction

always read introductions. I do not ever skip to the main part of the book without reading an introduction first, and my hope is that you will read this one.

This book is full of stories—God-stories that I never thought would be in print when I first began writing them down in March 2001.

The Lord had told me previously: "*John, lay down the right to write your stories.*"

You might say that was the death of a vision, but the morning the Lord told me to give up those stories, I got out of my truck, bowed my knee, and gave up the right to ever write or publish them. I drove away that day and forgot about it. The following December during a snow storm, I was just staring out the window when the Lord spoke to me:

"*John, I want you to write down the stories—get going!*"

So I did.

God must love stories; He put a lot of them in His book, the Bible. From Adam and Eve to Jonah and the whale to the stories in Acts and the hundreds in between, God uses stories to show us great spiritual truths.

After reading a rough draft of this book, my friend Mark Holmes asked me, "John, what's your goal for this book?"

Answer One: That Christians might know that they do not need to be "super saints" to hear the voice of the Lord. Jesus enjoys living in ordinary clay pots. The apostle Paul said in 2 Corinthians 4:7: "But we have this treasure in jars of clay to show that this all-surpassing power is from God and not from us" (NIV).

I also hope Christians would, by reading this book, find a renewed passion for Jesus.

Answer Two: That people who have not accepted Jesus as Lord of their lives will know the one true God and Jesus whom He sent, as it says in John 17:3: "Now this is eternal life: that they may know you, the only true God, and Jesus Christ, whom you have sent" (NIV).

The stories you are about to read are not about catching the ball with seven seconds left on the clock and running for the touchdown. They are not meant to draw attention to me or my life, which is why they aren't in chronological order. They are not part of a biography! These are stories that tell about a God who showed grace to a landscaper and then told the landscaper to share that grace with others. These stories reflect a life-walk with God. These stories are meant to bring Him glory and compel you to live so you do, too.

Some might say "Well, these are just experiences." To that I would say, "How right you are!" That is what life is: a walk of faith with Jesus, *experiences* with Jesus. That said, I also know that, as Peter said in 2 Peter 1:19, the more sure word is the Scriptures: "So we have the prophetic word made more sure, to which you do well to pay attention as to a lamp shining in a dark place, until the day dawns and the morning star arises in your hearts" (NAS).

Peter (along with James and John) had *experienced* the transfiguration of Christ, yet Peter still says the more sure word is the Scriptures, and to that I say amen!

At the end of each story are Scriptures and a question. Take time to meditate on the Scriptures, and ask yourself each question, giving an honest answer. My hope is that the Lord Jesus Christ will grant you the grace and the passion to seek Him with all your heart, soul, and mind, so when you have finished this book you might say along with the apostle Paul: "I want to know Christ and the power of his resurrection and the fellowship of sharing in his sufferings, becoming like him in his death, and so, somehow, to attain to the resurrection from the dead" (Philippians 3:10, NIV).

BLESSINGS, JOHN GORDON, APRIL, 2005

Hey, Mister

t was just another day in the landscape business. I had run around all day and, even though I have two gas tanks on my pickup, I had failed to notice that both tanks were on empty. While I generally fill up my vehicles at one or two stations, the situation required that I buy gas at a station across town at which I have never stopped before or since. Little did I know this experience with God would prove to be one of my most treasured.

The pumps were about fifty feet from the convenience store. I thought, *I'll just put in five dollars worth of gas and go.* When I went in to pay for my gas, I had to stand in line because the store clerk was trying to help two kids who were counting out pennies, nickels, and dimes. They were purchasing some items—milk and bread and such—that made me assume their mom had sent them to the store.

While I was waiting, I watched the two children. The little girl was about nine years old with strawberry-blonde hair and a ruddy complexion. The little boy, whom I assumed was her brother, looked like he was several years younger. They both had matted hair and dirty clothes. I got the impression that they took care of their mom more than she took care of them.

The line in the store was getting longer, and the store clerk was getting impatient with the two kids. The little girl finished paying for the items and then turned to her brother.

"You think we got 'nuff money to buy a pop?" she asked him in a twangy voice. The little boy put his hands in his pockets and shrugged his shoulders. The store clerk had had enough and told the two to move along. They went outside.

I tossed my five dollars on the counter, grabbed the receipt, and walked outside. That's when He showed up like so many times before. I heard that wonderful voice say, "*John, I want those two kids to have a pop.*" I immediately turned to look for them and, sure enough, huddled by the ice machine, were the two children, still trying to count their change.

"Young lady, come over here," I called. The little girl looked up at me, but as she came over, she had her head down like she thought she was in trouble. "Look up here at me," I said. "Jesus wants you and your brother to have a pop. Here's two dollars; go get whatever you want."

I handed her the money and started walking to my truck. I had almost reached it when I heard someone running after me. I turned around, and there stood that little girl. She looked up at me with the biggest smile on her face.

"Hey, mister," she said, "would you tell Him I said thank you?"

I was surprised and felt myself choke up. "I'll be sure to tell Him," I promised.

I drove out of that parking lot with tears streaming down my face. I thought, *How many times do we forget to say thank you? How many times do we forget to have a grateful and thankful attitude for all that God has done for us?*

> As Jesus continued on toward Jerusalem, he reached the border between Galilee and Samaria. As He entered a village there, ten lepers stood at a distance crying out, "Jesus, Master, have mercy on us!" He looked at them and said, "Go, show yourselves to the priests." And as they went, they were cleansed of their leprosy. One of them, when he saw that he was healed, came back to Jesus, shouting, "Praise God!" He fell to the ground at Jesus' feet, thanking Him for what He had done. This man was a Samaritan. Jesus asked, "Didn't I heal ten men? Where are the other nine? Has no one returned to give glory to God except this foreigner? And Jesus said to the man, "Stand up and go. Your faith has healed you."
>
> LUKE 17:11–19 (NLT)

*Give thanks in all circumstances, for this is God's will for you in
Christ Jesus.*

1 THESSALONIANS 5:18 (NIV)

Being Honest with Myself:

Do I have a thankful heart?

The Man in Blue Jeans and the
Newly-Elected Congressman

My wife and I made a trip to Atlanta back in the early 1980s to attend a conference at Dr. Charles Stanley's church. The Lord had worked in our lives in a deep way, and we were anxious to attend any conference that would feed our insatiable appetite for the things God was teaching us.

While in Georgia, we stayed with my parents, who lived in Roswell. At that time my sister and her husband lived nearby in Atlanta. My brother-in-law, Rick, had just been through an extremely busy year at the helm of his friend's campaign for Congress in Dunwoody, Georgia. This had been an uphill battle because they were trying to unseat an incumbent with over ten years of experience under his belt. My brother-in-law was a brilliant strategist and had won the election for his friend Pat. So Pat was the newly-elected congressman from Dunwoody. Pat was the essence of what one would imagine a congressman to be. He was young, energetic, and handsome. He had a brilliant mind for the law, much like Rick, and both of them had practiced in the Peach state.

Late one Georgia evening, my wife asked me to go to the store for diapers and formula. I was tired from the conference and asked, "Sweetheart, can't it wait until morning?"

"No, it can't," she replied.

So I put on my shoes, grabbed her list, and drove to Kroger's in Roswell. No one was in the store except some sleepy workers and me. My intention was to quickly get what I needed and go. Not being familiar with the store, I found myself wandering endlessly to find the things I needed.

As I was standing staring at the list, trying to match the items to the signs above the aisles, I noticed a tall man walking toward me, dressed to the nines—Pat, the newly-elected congressman. He did not know me, and I only knew him from photos from the *Atlanta Constitution*, which my sister had shown me. I thought, *What the heck, I might as well walk up and say 'Hi.'*

"Hi. Aren't you Pat?" I asked.

"Yes, I am."

"My name is John Gordon," I said, "and my brother-in-law is Rick, your business partner and campaign manager." With that I caught his attention.

"Rick has done a wonderful job," Pat said ardently.

"I'm sure he has," I replied. We made some more small talk, but both of us were tired. I started to walk away. Then the Lord spoke to me. "*John*," the Lord said, "*There is something I want you to tell Pat.*" I stopped and turned.

"Pat, hold on a second, I want to tell you something," I said, and relayed the message I felt the Lord wanted him to hear. "Pat, when you get to Washington, D.C., walk uprightly before the Lord, do what is right, and don't compromise your values."

As we began to part company again, the Lord said to me, "*Tell him one more time.*"

I grabbed his arm, looked him straight in the eye, and said, "Pat, the Lord is impressing me to tell you one more time: walk uprightly before God when you get to Washington, D.C." With a disgusted "I-heard-you-the-first-time" attitude, he pulled his arm away, turned, and walked down the dairy aisle.

I never saw Pat again, except in the paper. He went off to Washington, the newly-elected congressman. At the time, the F.B.I was doing undercover sting operations. The undercover agents met Pat in a discrete location, and he accepted hundreds of thousands of dollars in bribes. I understand that three days later he tried to give the money back, but it was too late. He was exposed and humiliated. Pat lost his seat in Congress.

Then the word of the Lord came to Samuel: "I am grieved that I have made Saul king, because he has turned away from me and has not carried out my instructions."

1 SAMUEL 15:10–11 (NIV)

A good name is more desirable than great riches; to be esteemed is better than silver or gold.

PROVERBS 22:1 (NIV)

Being Honest with Myself:

Am I a person of godly character?

The Glory

Between the years of 1972 and 1986, I worked for the Lily Tulip Corporation. I was simply a factory worker who ran a machine. My life was not easy, but God wanted me there.

The part of the plant in which I worked manufactured a foam cup. The factory was hot, sometimes unbearable, as the machines had ovens that were heated to over a thousand degrees. I can remember many nights seeing people drop as temperatures climbed to over 120 degrees. Everything was dirty; dust filled the air. The noise was unbearable without earplugs.

One advantage of my job was that the company wanted optimum production. As long as I could keep the equipment running, I had time to read. I have always loved a good book. Although I favor John Grisham, I tend to read books that lean toward the spiritual: authors like Yancey, Stanley, MacArthur, Rogers, Blackaby, and Piper.

One particular evening, I was reading a book by Jack Taylor, the former President of the Southern Baptist Convention. I've forgotten the title; the book has long since disappeared from my bookshelves, but what I am about to tell you will never slip my memory. In his book, Jack Taylor was telling the story of an old evangelist by the name of Dwight L. Moody. Mr. Moody was walking down the street in New York City, and the Spirit of the living God fell on him. The Spirit of God was so strong that he stayed in his room for several days as God's Spirit baptized him. According to the book, from that day on, his ministry was never the same.

Sitting there in that dirty factory, I started contemplating the story I had just read. Finally, I said, "Lord, what is it like to be in the presence of your glory?"

I can only ask for grace to convey what happened next. In the bowels of that dirt-filled factory, the presence of God fell on me. While it would be wrong to say I saw anything, I was allowed to enter a realm that I will never forget. The joy I experienced is beyond human description. I lost my voice and could not speak as the glory of the great God engulfed me. Time seemed to stand still, and my surroundings became like one looking into an aquarium.

His wonderful Spirit and my spirit became one in a way that I cannot adequately describe. As this happened, I realized that my spirit wanted to leave my body. I wanted to go be with Him forever. I am not sure how I knew this, but at that point I knew I was dying.

Now mind you, this was not a terrible thing. On the contrary, it was exhilarating beyond explanation. The whole time my mind was quite alert, and I remember thinking, *Lord, I'm going to die if you don't go*. Ever so gently, the Lord slipped out of the Lily Tulip factory that night. My last thought was from Him: *"John, that was just the touch of the hem of my garment."*

Up to this point, I have only told a few people this story. Because of this experience, I know exactly what King David meant when he penned the words in Psalm 27:4 (NIV):

> *One thing I ask of the Lord, this is what I seek: that I may dwell in the house of the Lord all the days of my life, to gaze upon the beauty of the Lord and to seek him in his temple.*

I cannot wait to see Jesus and live in the presence of God. I am saddened when I think of how few people seem to have a deep yearning to be with God.

> *Dear friends, now we are children of God, and what we will be has not yet been made known. But we know that when He appears, we shall be like Him, for we shall see Him as He is.*
>
> 1 JOHN 3:2 (NIV)

And [Moses] said, "Please show me your glory." And God did.
[emphasis and postscript mine]

EXODUS 33:18 (NKJV)

Being Honest with Myself:

Do I really look forward to meeting Jesus, and if not, why?

The Vision

Fasting is something I have done periodically since 1986. In 1997, I had just finished a ten day fast. I was sitting alone at home when the presence of God came into my living room. Now, I am not one given to grandstanding, and I certainly do not want to convey to anyone that I went into a trance or something. However, as clearly as I can see with my physical eyes, the Lord began to show me a vision with spiritual eyes. Here is that vision:

I walked into a big department store, the most fabulous store I had ever seen. The store was nicer and bigger than Bloomingdale's or Saks Fifth Avenue in New York City. I could not see the end of it. Thousands of sales clerks offered everything imaginable. Wealth could be purchased at one counter; thousands of people were pushing and shoving just to get up to that counter. Power was also available; thousands more pressed against one another to get to the clerks in charge. The most beautiful houses, boats, and cars were in this store, all of which were being hawked by savvy store personnel. Beauty was there, fame, anything one's heart would desire. I saw a huge part of this store dedicated to sexual fantasies. The knowledge section of the store was filled with every kind of philosophy, religion, and book ever conceived by the mind of man.

Walking around the store, I, too, found myself enthralled. I began to feel pulled to one counter after another. Getting up to an open spot at the counters was difficult; when I asked the price, I realized the cost in this store was astronomical. Some of the things I could purchase would cost me my family. Other things would cost me my health. Still others would cost me my soul. I turned away from each one, not wanting to pay such a high price, only to be quickly tempted by another option.

While wandering around the store with thousands of people pushing and shoving their way around, I felt a hand on my shoulder. I turned, and it was Jesus. He simply said, "John, I will show you the best thing in the store if you will follow me." With all the commotion still going on around me, I thought, *Okay, Lord, I'll follow.*

"Lord," I said, "Where are we going?"

"Back there," Jesus said, simply. I hadn't noticed it until He pointed it out to me, but way back in the store, as far as I could see, was a beautiful light. I asked what it was.

"That is the glory of God," He said.

"Lord, how do I get there?" I asked.

He replied: "I'll show you; you follow me."

At His bidding, I walked with Him. We did not go very far until He stopped and offered someone else the very same thing that He had offered me. That person's response was "Don't bother me right now." Every so often, He would stop and ask people to follow Him. Some would go with Him, while others would not even acknowledge His presence.

I have to admit that as we walked the path to the glory of God, every now and then I would look over at the different sales counters to see what was available. Each time, I would feel His hand on my shoulder, and He would remind me that what He has to offer is much better, and as long as I continued to follow Him, He would show me the glory.

I have never forgotten that vision, and I know I never will. Let me encourage you today that when He beckons you, push yourself away from whatever counter you may be up against and follow Him. You will be glad you did.

> *Do not love the world or anything in the world. If anyone loves the world, the love of the Father is not in him.*
>
> 1 JOHN 2:15 (NIV)

And anyone who does not carry his cross and follow me cannot be my disciple.

LUKE 14:27 (NIV)

Being Honest with Myself:

What do I love more than the Lord?

The Beginning of a Prayer Life

Prayer . . . what an interesting concept. Many books have been written about prayer, and the subject has been explored from every angle possible. It is not my intention to provide new insight. Rather, I would like to tell the story of my own beginning on the prayer journey.

Spring of 1988 was a busy time for my wife and me. We had to hurry to get the greenhouses open. That kind of work is just that: a lot of work. But we did that amount of work in a short period of time, hoping the rewards would equal the effort. Fourteen-to-sixteen hour days were not uncommon during this ten-week period.

The point I am making is that we lived a tired life for those ten weeks. So one night, when the wonderful voice of God awoke me at 4:30 a.m., I cannot tell you that I leapt to my feet and stood at attention. I remember just crawling out of bed and standing there, mumbling, "Yes, sir."

"*John, get your clothes on and go out to the golf course*," the Lord said. I knew which golf course He meant, since I often played at Fremont Hills Country Club with friends.

I put my clothes on, jumped in the car, and drove to the golf course to hear what God wanted to tell me. Once I was there, I did not know where to go. Finally I drove back by the fourth tee box, a place out of the way. Back then, no houses had been built around that area.

I parked the car and got out. I walked over to the tee box, looked up to Heaven, and asked, "What do you want to say, Lord?" His response surprised me.

"John," He said, "*you are not low enough to hear.*"

I considered that for a few seconds and thought maybe I needed to kneel down. Just then, the Lord spoke again.

"*John, put your face in that hole.*" I knelt down and put my face in a hole next to the tee box.

"*Now you are low enough to hear me,*" God said. "*John, I am calling you to pray at 4:30 every morning. You can stand before my throne and minister to me.*"

All I could do was weep.

Truthfully, back then I did not understand the full meaning of what the Lord had said to me. Even today, with sixteen years of coming before that glorious throne hundreds and hundreds of mornings, I still think, *why me?*

I wish I could say that I have never missed a morning in sixteen years, but I cannot, and once when I tried taking a sabbatical, I was chastened! I'll explain further in the next chapter. However, I do not miss many mornings, and I can tell you that I would not trade those mornings for anything this world has to offer. God might not expect you to pray at 4:30 in the morning, but He does expect you to find your personal "prayer closet" sometime during the day.

I do not know what it is like to be able to walk into the President's office or that of any other leader or dignitary. But I can tell you what it is like to stand in the presence of the Glorious One, the King of Kings and Lord of Lords. I can tell you what it is like to hear Him say, *Good morning, John; I am glad you are here!*

> *Who may ascend the hill of the Lord? Who may stand in His holy place? He who has clean hands and a pure heart, who does not lift up his soul to an idol or swear by what is false. He will receive blessing from the Lord and vindication from God his Savior. Such is the generation of those who seek him, who seek your face, O God of Jacob.*
>
> PSALM 24:3–6 (NIV)

> *The eyes of the Lord watch over those who do right, and his ears are open to their prayers.*
>
> 1 PETER 3:12 (NLT)

How blessed is the one whom You choose and bring near to You To dwell in Your courts . . .

PSALM 65:4 (NAS)

Being Honest with Myself:

How would my prayer life rate with the Lord?

The Accident that
Was No Accident

I t would be nice if every story were a pleasant one, but of course since we are human, that can never be.

In the late 1980s, I felt the call of the Lord to devote more time to prayer. So, along with several others, a 4:30 a.m. prayer meeting was birthed. That went along for a while until people began dropping out or moving along. We found ourselves moving from one location to another, with each move bringing fewer people. After about three years of getting up at 4:30, I started growing weary. Finally, I made the decision to quit for a while. Mind you, I only intended to leave for a small sabbatical. To my friend Ed's credit, he warned me: "John, I don't think you should do this." But my mind was made up; I needed a break, and I decided that someone else could carry the ball.

This decision turned into a slide, then a fall, to the point that I became disinterested in the important things and more interested in worldly pursuits. I do not want to imply that I was on a big sinning program or something, but I was not interested in what was important to the Lord. I thought I would get back to spiritual things "later."

About six months into my new attitude, I was test-driving a small Toyota pickup truck that a friend of mine owned and wanted to sell. The weather that day was rainy and windy. I thought I would take the truck out on the four-lane highway to see how it handled, then cut back across the country by Lake Springfield before driving back home. While driving across the dam that day, I can only tell you that what happened was a supernatural experience. As though an invisible hand reached down and gave that truck a shove, off I went into a spin about one hundred feet across the little dam. The truck got almost to the end of the dam and back on the road when I heard the Lord's voice with a sternness in it that I do not often hear.

"*John*," He said, "*I'd like to talk to you for a minute.*"

Upon hearing His voice, I remember shouting, "Lord, help me!" He did not respond immediately; the truck continued to spin until it fell off an embankment about 150 feet from the end of the dam. The truck was pinned against a tree about thirty feet above a small cliff; I could see a limb one foot from my head. I was scared to death that limb would break, causing me to flip end over end. At that moment, He spoke.

"*John, you have taken Me for granted. Come back to Me.*"

The Lord did not have to say anything more. I knew I had let other things in life become too significant, more important than Him. Within a few minutes that day, a couple on their way to work saw me pinned there against the tree, shouted at me to make sure I was okay, and then called for a tow truck. But I did not soon forget what the Lord had said to me. I did not want to take Him for granted again.

In the book of Jonah is a story of a man who decided he was not going to do what God told him to do. Instead of a Toyota truck, God used a big whale to get Jonah's attention. Have you taken flight from what you know you should be doing, somewhere you know you should be going? Don't make the Lord send a truck after you.

> *My son, do not despise the Lord's discipline and do not resent his rebuke, because the Lord disciplines those he loves, as a father the son he delights in.*
>
> PROVERBS 3:11–12 (NIV)

> *. . . I've got my eye on the goal, where God is beckoning us onward—to Jesus. I'm off and running, and I'm not turning back.*
>
> PHILIPPIANS 3:14 (THE MESSAGE)

Being Honest with Myself:

Have I taken the Lord for granted?

My Scariest Moment with God

"J ohn, can you help me?" said my friend, Jack, on the other end of the phone.

"Well, I don't know. What's the problem?" I said.

My friend Jack had gotten into a business that I knew little to nothing about. He had been catapulted to a high position in the company. With the job came all the typical perks, plus a significant six-figure income. But Jack said he was having trouble with work and was wondering if he could "pick my brain." We set a breakfast meeting for the following morning.

I met him the next morning as planned. I told him up front that I did not know anything about his business, but that I would talk with him and help if I could. As he explained his problem, I knew the situation was dire, but I could see a way out if he took certain steps that involved more "people skills" than "business skills."

Jack had acquired a lot of the toys that come with a well-paying job. He had a nice family, and frankly, God had been good to him. However, Jack lacked one thing, which I kept reminding him of throughout the morning. Over and over I heard the Lord speaking to me, saying, *John, tell him the goodness of God leads to repentance. Tell him I want him to commit his life to Me.*

Jack was not interested, but in all my years the Lord has never been this persistent. I would hear Him say, *John, tell him again!* I would say, "Jack, look, I'm not trying to bug you, but I keep hearing God tell me that he wants you to commit your life to Him *today*!"

For about three hours, I gave what advice I could and pleaded with this man to accept Christ into his life. No time before or since have I felt the heart of God in this manner as God begged this man through me to give his life to Him. I finally decided to call it quits and leave. He asked me if I would ride with him back to his house, so I did.

As we pulled into his driveway, I felt the Lord tell me to give it everything I could, to call out to Jack in one last desperate attempt to get him to respond to the gospel. Jack looked disgusted because I kept pressing the issue, and he simply said, "Not now." We walked into his house.

Even now I find it difficult to write about what happened next. As we entered the house, one of Jack's children was doing something he found irritating. He started blaspheming the name of God over and over again. At that point, I heard the Lord say, "*I am finished with this man. I will never deal with him again!*" I felt, yes *felt*, the Spirit of God depart.

In my life, I have never felt that kind of fear, as if God were literally showing me what it would be like to hear Jesus say, "Depart from me; I never knew you." I will tell you this: I understand Paul's words in 2 Corinthians 5:11, "Knowing, therefore, the terror of the Lord, we persuade men . . ." (NKJV). Has God been calling you? Have you been invited by the Holy Spirit to make a decision for Christ? Has the wonderful person of the Holy Spirit been wooing you? You must come, and come quickly.

> *Blessed is the man who always fears the Lord, but he who hardens his heart falls into trouble.*
>
> PROVERBS 28:14 (NIV)

> *So, as the Holy Spirit says: 'Today, if you hear his voice, do not harden your hearts as you did in the rebellion, during the time of testing in the desert . . ."*
>
> HEBREWS 3:7–8 (NIV)

Being Honest with Myself:

Have I hardened my heart toward the Lord in any way?

God's Friend

would have to say that I hear the Lord best when I am alone with Him. I have probably heard God's voice more in my truck or in the shower than I have anywhere else. I have also gotten accustomed to hearing God's voice when I least expect it.

In the summer of 1998, I was running at the usual busy pace that the landscaping business brings. I had to make a fast trip to Ava, Missouri, to pick up a load of mulch for a job that needed to be finished that day. Although the day itself was ordinary, my experience with God that day probably means more to me than any other.

I had just left Seymour from a rest stop and was headed east to Mansfield when, at the junction of Cedar Gap and Highway 60, the Spirit of God came into my truck. I began to weep; His presence was so real. I had nothing to say; the tears kept me from talking. Then, with a gentleness and deep emotion, I heard the Lord speak to my heart.

"*John*," He said, "*I want you to know that you are My friend.*"

Me! I thought, *God's friend?* It seemed unimaginable. I wept all the way to Ava.

I bought my mulch and headed back home, still reeling from those words: *John, you are My friend.* When I got back to almost the same area of the highway, the presence of the Lord came again into my truck. This time, however, the Lord asked me a question.

"*John*," He said, "*am I your friend?*"

"Yes, Lord! Yes, Lord! You are!" I cried, "You're my best friend, better even than Brenda, my Redhead."

And to this day, even years later, He's still the best friend I have. I can tell you that nothing I can think of could mean more to me than the great God telling insignificant me, "John, you are my friend." I have thought about it a lot since then. I often ask for the grace to love Him more than anything else, period.

To be a friend is to share everything, to listen, to care more about your friend's interests than you might your own. Hundreds of times I have said to Him, "God, make me the best friend to You that I can be." I want Him to look down on the earth and be able to say that no one loves Him more than His friend, John.

What do you desire in this world? I hope it is to hear God call you His friend.

> *I no longer call you servants, because a servant does not know his master's business. Instead, I have called you friends, for everything that I learned from my Father I have made known to you.*
>
> JOHN 15:15 (NIV)

Being Honest with Myself:

Do I consider God my friend?
Do I love Him more than anyone or anything?

Five Days in Arkansas

For three or four months in the fall of 2000, I kept hearing the Lord say, *"John, I want you to go off and be with Me alone."* I told my wife I would stay home until after New Years Day, then I would go spend time alone with God. I did not know where I would go; I just knew I was going.

At first I thought I might go to Colorado, but that was more miles than I wanted to drive. I looked into two monasteries: one in Ava, Missouri, and one run by John Michael Talbott in Eureka Springs, Arkansas. Neither of those worked out. Finally, my friend Sparky suggested I stay at his parents' place in Malvern, Arkansas. His folks, John and Bonita Cunningham, graciously agreed; there was a small cabin behind their house that would be my home away from home for my stay in Malvern. I headed south about 250 miles to stay for however long God kept me there.

Armed with juice, which I usually drink diluted during a fast, quite a few books, the Bible (of course!), and several notebooks, I settled in at the cabin to hear God. The first night I thought I would pray before going to bed, but I could not think of anything to say. *Oh well,* I thought, *I must be tired. I'll hit it in the morning.* Off to sleep I went. The next day, instead of things getting better, they got worse. I could not hear God. I did not feel His presence. I could not pray. Nothing!

I resorted to taking long walks with John and Bonita's big, black Labrador Retriever. Malvern had been hit with what might have been the worst ice storm in the history of that town. I do not know that for sure, but except for the snow and ice everywhere, the whole town looked like a tornado had hit. I would walk for several miles through the snow each day. God was not talking, so I would come back to the cabin with nothing. I can't say the same for that dog; he brought something back from different yards after every walk!

About the fourth day, I started thinking I had made a mistake (the Lord knows I have made more than my fair share). I decided to go into town with John Cunningham to get the grand tour of Hot Springs, Arkansas. I thought I would go home and simply tell my wife Brenda that I blew this one. But I just couldn't. I thought, *I'll stay one more day.*

That night I thought I would read a little book that the James Robinson organization had sent me called *The Prayer of Jabez.* I had not heard of it at the time. It is fairly short, so I thought I could read it in a few hours. Well, all I remember next is waking up the next morning, the book lying on the bed beside me and still feeling spiritually as cold as the weather outside. I was going into my fifth day without food, sitting there alone in that cabin, watching the birds, thinking, *I oughtta go home.* Well . . . tomorrow anyway. I didn't feel like driving at night. So I picked up that little book with the intention of finishing it that evening. I got to the very last page around 7:30 p.m. on Saturday. On that page was printed the prayer of Jabez, found in 1 Chronicles 4:10 (NIV):

> *Jabez cried out to the God of Israel, "Oh, that you would bless me and enlarge my territory! Let your hand be with me, and keep me from harm so that I will be free from pain." And God granted his request.*

That is when He came. The great King, my Friend. His glory flooded the room. He said, *"John, put your name there: 'John cried out to the God of Israel . . . ' I have heard you and will do this in your life."*

I spent the next five hours worshipping the Savior of my soul. I wept and worshipped and praised that night as His spirit flooded my soul. Waves of glory swept through that room until I was so exhausted, I fell sound asleep. I woke up Sunday morning to His wonderful voice as He said, *"John, you may go home. I have heard you."*

Quite frankly, I still am not sure what God meant or what He has planned, but I do know that 1 Thessalonians 5:24 says: "The one who calls you is faithful and he will do it" (NIV). Do what? Make you like Jesus!

What has God told you He will do with your life? Do you believe Him—even when that promise doesn't happen tomorrow, next week, or next year? Wait for Him to fulfill the dream He has for your life. He wants to bless you with every spiritual blessing. And if you have not heard from on high lately, maybe you need to call home.

You do not have, because you do not ask God.

—JAMES 4:2 (NIV)

I turned to the Master God, asking for an answer—praying earnestly, fasting from meals, wearing rough penitential burlap, and kneeling in the ashes. I poured out my heart, baring my soul to God, my God . . .

DANIEL 9:3 (THE MESSAGE)

Being Honest with Myself:

Have I ever set aside a time to seek the Lord?

Gypsy Rose Lee

This story reflects one of my first experiences with God. I do not remember the year, but back in the 1960s, my parents, my two siblings, and I lived in Danville, Kentucky. My dad was gone on the road a lot, and my mom was a homemaker.

Now, there was certainly no doubt about the fact that my mom was a staunch Christian. There was no gray in the woman; everything was black or white, right or wrong, and the word "compromise" did not enter her thinking. She taught me three things: the Bible, Aesop's fables, and catchy sayings.

Unless we were dying (and that was her call), we went to church on Sunday morning, Sunday night, and Wednesday night. We took a cab if Dad was not at home and we could not get a ride with a friend because my mother didn't drive. I can remember many a time ducking down in the seat of the cab because I thought it was silly. It did not matter; "The church doors are open," she would say.

Danville was a small town then, and safe. So I could ride my bike anywhere. Mom did not care, but she would have me call to tell her when I would be home for supper. Saturday was movie day; if the movie was good and clean, I could go. If Mom did not deem it okay, it was a no-go. Period.

One Friday, my friend Rich asked me to go to the movie the next day with him.

"Okay," I said, "What's on?" He told me it was a movie called "Gypsy Rose Lee."

"What's that about?" I asked.

"It's about a stripper!" Rich whispered. "See you tomorrow!"

I did not feel right about going—it is called a conscience—but I fought it off as best I could. The next morning, I told Mom I was going to see a friend.

I paid the money, got my Black Cow candy bar, and went in to see Natalie Wood in "Gypsy Rose Lee." I had only been there about thirty minutes when an usher walked down the aisle and loudly announced: "John Gordon, your mother is in the lobby and wants to see you right now!"

My heart sank. I got physically sick to my stomach. I walked out into the lobby and saw my mom. With no expression whatsoever, she said, "Johnny, you'd better be home before the cab driver gets me home."

The Ivory soap tasted terrible; the grounding was worse. But God spoke through her that day. Mom walked in my room that night, looked me straight in the eye, and said, "Son, do right 'til the stars fall. Go eat your supper."

There will always be people who want to lead you astray. There will always be a wrong road to go down. Don't go . . .

> No temptation has seized you except what is common to man. And God is faithful; he will not let you be tempted beyond what you can bear. But when you are tempted, he will also provide a way out so that you can stand up under it.
>
> 1 CORINTHIANS 10:13 (NIV)

> Be strong and very courageous. Be careful to obey all the law my servant Moses gave you; do not turn from it to the right or to the left, that you may be successful wherever you go.
>
> JOSHUA 1:7 (NIV)

Being Honest with Myself:

Do I walk as closely to the line as possible? Do I justify ungodly behavior?

A Day in Toronto

ach year around our wedding anniversary in mid-June, I try to take a break from the landscape business and get away with my wife. The destinations vary, and, being a person who looks for good deals, I am not always sure where we will end up. One summer we were planning to vacation in Toronto, Canada. Our great friends, Sparky and Toni, graciously went with us.

Canada is beautiful in the summer and, having never been to Niagara Falls, we had settled on Toronto as our destination. We were scheduled to be there for five days at the Sheraton Hotel. We would be able to drive to see the sights or have the option of walking around in Toronto.

For me, the mornings were spent in the lobby, nursing a Starbucks coffee, praying, and reading. I was always downstairs by about 5:30 a.m. with book, Bible, and Walkman. I would try to spend two hours with Jesus before I started the day. On the third morning, I was reading *Secrets of the Vine* by Bruce Wilkinson, which I was enjoying even more than the first book of his I had read. I sensed God deeply stirring my soul. At first I thought maybe that was due to the 1,300 gays and lesbians that had arrived at the hotel for the world conference of Metropolitan Community Churches. I do not think I have ever felt so alone with so many people around. Most of the Metropolitan leaders who started to sit around me would look at my Bible and the book I was reading, stare at me for a moment, then pick up the furniture, move it to another part of the lobby, and leave me sitting alone. That was fine . . . but it was a very different feeling than you get in southwest Missouri.

This particular morning, I could not get away from the fact that God was moving. His presence got so strong that I decided to walk and pray out in the hotel's garden courtyard. After I had walked around several times, the spirit of God came like a flood. He said to me, *"John, would you give up one of your vacation days and spend it with me?"* His presence swept over me. I finally thought I had better go to my room to be with God alone. That was about 7:30 a.m., and for six hours God and I stayed in that room. Not one time did He ask me to do anything. Not one time did I ask Him for anything. I worshipped and He never said much more than *"John, I am glad you are My friend."*

Around 1:30 in the afternoon, He said to me: *"You're getting hungry; I'm going for now. I love you, son."*

"I love you, too, Lord!" I answered. Then my stomach started talking to me.

> *Very early in the morning, while it was still dark, Jesus got up, left the house and went off to a solitary place, where he prayed.*
>
> MARK 1:35 (NIV)

Being Honest with Myself:

Do I make it a point to be alone with God? What keeps me from spending quality time alone with the High and Holy One?

Senior English Class

My senior year in high school was 1969–1970. I had attended six schools since junior high, and I was spending my last year at Wade Hampton High in Greenville, South Carolina. Wade Hampton was a large school; my graduating class included over nine hundred students. I had only one good friend at that school, a guy who worked out with me constantly.

I was always pretty good in school, except for my struggles with English class. My senior English teacher was . . . different. I remember the first week of class, his first question was, "How many of you believe there is a God?" About half of the class raised their hands, including me. I saw why he asked that later; that whole year, all he had us read were books about communism, socialism, existentialism, and Hinduism.

At the end of the year, my grades were hovering close to failing. I attributed this to not caring for the questions on the tests he would give, and I hated reading the books. My attitude toward him was poor as well; it seemed to me he went out of his way to mock God.

On the last day of class, my teacher walked in and asked the same question he had in the beginning: "How many of you believe there is a God?"

The Lord said to me, *"John, how about it?"* Only two people in the class raised their hands: a girl on the other side of the room, and me. That man had convinced over half his students to doubt or forsake their convictions.

We live in a world that goes out of its way to deny God His rightful place. Let me encourage you to be bold for Christ, for He said in

Matthew 10:32–33: "Whoever acknowledges me before men, I will also acknowledge him before my Father in heaven. But whoever disowns me before men, I will disown him before my Father in heaven" (NIV). The world will give you a thousand reasons not to believe; voices come from every direction. Let me encourage you always to be bold, and believe in the one who has called you.

> *But there were also false prophets among the people, even as there will be false teachers among you, who will secretly bring in destructive heresies, even denying the Lord who bought them, and bring on themselves swift destruction.*
>
> 2 PETER 2:1 (NKJV)

> *Let your conversation be always full of grace, seasoned with salt, so that you may know how to answer everyone.*
>
> COLOSSIANS 4:6 (NIV)

Being Honest with Myself:

Do I speak up for Jesus, or am I ashamed and embarrassed when the subject turns to my Lord?

Angry with God

My wife and I were in our mid-twenties when she had our first child. I do not remember being prepared, but we looked forward to the birth of our son. March of 1977 rolled around, and all the babies from our Lamaze class had been born. Finally, two and a half weeks past the due date, we brought home our son, Chris. He was bright-eyed and very observant. He was quite a beautiful child. Like all parents, we were happy to show him off.

About nine to eleven months into his life, we started noticing that he could not hold his head up straight, and he did not seem to respond to our voices the way he should. We kept thinking he was just late to develop; maybe he was a little slower than most kids, but surely he would come around. When he was a little over one year old, relatives started commenting on his lack of progress. My wife and I thought maybe we should get him checked by a physician. The first doctor said he thought Chris had cerebral palsy. We thought we should get a second opinion. The next doctor thought Chris had a mild case of mental retardation.

As you can imagine, the next several months were difficult. We watched the kids in church begin to walk and talk. However, we had made up our minds that Chris was just slow and he would catch up. For those few months, we put our heads in the sand. God surely would not give us a handicapped child! Why, He is a good God!

As we got to the 16 to 18 month stage, there was no denying that something was wrong with our son. He still could not walk, he could not talk, he could not hold his head up, and he was deathly afraid of the dark. When we drove around the city, we always drove on streets with streetlights, never where it was dark. Finally, my mother-in-law said she felt that Chris could not hear. We made one more doctor's appointment with a hearing specialist. They gave Chris an audiogram, which they said did not look good, and they suggested we get a second opinion at the Central Institute for the Deaf at Washington University in St. Louis, Missouri.

We made the appointment and went to St. Louis. We knew full well that Chris had a *little* problem . . . but there were hearing aids. God would never allow something worse to happen to us. I will never forget the outcome of that St. Louis trip.

"Mr. and Mrs. Gordon—your son is profoundly deaf."

That is all I remember hearing that day. I went numb. Neither my wife nor I had ever known a deaf person. What did that mean? Surely a place like Washington University could fix this.

"We are sorry," they told us, "your son has severe hearing loss. There is nothing we can do except fit him with hearing aids . . . but they probably won't help him much at all."

I could not think. My wife went into shock. We walked back to our car not saying a word. Both of us felt sick.

Our friends who lived in St. Louis graciously let us spend the night. I remember when my wife went to bed, I sat down alone at the kitchen table to think about what I had just been told. *God, why? What have we done to deserve this? It's not fair! Brenda and I have tried to live a decent Christian life. Why did you do this to us? Why did you let it happen?* As I sat there, my anger finally came to a boiling point, and I slammed my fist down on the table and shouted,

"God, I hate you for this! We don't deserve this!"

That was September, 1978, and I did not darken the door of a church until 1980. I completely shut God out. If He wanted to treat Brenda and me like this, I didn't need Him.

I am not mad at God anymore, but my attitude did not change back overnight. It took over two years for God to get it through my head. He was not mad, but like Job, I had to come to a place where I realized God has the right to be God.

Maybe like me, your child was born handicapped. Maybe you

THE LORD AND THE LANDSCAPER

were abused. Maybe your husband or wife ran off with someone else. Maybe a business went south or a company did you wrong after you gave them years of loyal service. But the question is still the same: are you offended at God? Are you displeased with the way God allowed something to happen to you? Isaiah 45 talks about contending with our Maker. Let me assure you that God is a good God. Calamities and bad things are going to happen in this fallen world, but our Heavenly Father is there to save and comfort.

> God said, "And who do you think made the human mouth? And who makes some mute, some deaf, some sighted, some blind? Isn't it I, God?"
>
> EXODUS 4:11 (THE MESSAGE)

> "Do you presume to tell me what I'm doing wrong? Are you calling me a sinner so you can be a saint?"
>
> JOB 40:8 (THE MESSAGE)

Being Honest with Myself:

Am I upset with God?

Am I angry about family, illness, position, or many things?

Frank

During the early to late 1970s, I was on a pilgrimage of sorts. I had become disillusioned with church, religion, and denominations. I was just tired of it all. I had been told my whole life to love God, to keep His commandments, and not to miss church. People encouraged me to hang in there and not let go of my faith. They said Jesus would be coming back soon. Now there is nothing wrong with church, religion, loving God, or wanting Jesus to come back. But for me, it did not fill the void. Eventually, I started going to Christian counseling with Bill and Annabel Gilham, who were and are wonderful, gifted people.

I guess you would have to say that I became a disciple of the Gilhams and Chuck and Sue Soloman, both of whom were teaching the "Exchanged Life Principles." The problem was that, although I knew in my spirit that these teachers were right, I felt it was not happening for me. I could not connect. All the while, problems such as finances, marriage difficulties, a child with special needs, and my own inner turmoil hovered over me like a dark cloud every day.

One day I was talking to a friend of mine who was dealing with some marriage problems of his own. He told me about a man in Harrison, Arkansas, named Frank, a simple farmer who also counseled people. I thought, *I might as well go.* So my wife and I went to see him and discuss our problems with marriage, our son, and other life issues. I didn't go with the best of attitudes, but I went. Frank spent hours with us talking about Christ being our life, quoting Galatians 2:20 until he was blue in the face.

"Frank," we would say, "we came to discuss our marriage, our child, and our innermost feelings!"

"I know," he would say, "but that's not your problem; your problem is that you need Christ at the center of your life! John, you need His life; He's the one who overcame the world, and He can live through you in victory!" All the while, my life was falling apart.

The thing about Frank was that I knew he loved me, and deep down I knew that what he said was right, but I wondered if I would ever experience those answers in my life. God granted me that knowledge on January 3, 1980, when I finally understood what Frank meant when he kept quoting Galatians 2:20: God did not expect me to live the Christian life; that would only result in failure. What He asked was for me to be willing to let Christ live through me. That day was the biggest milestone in my life. That day, God let me start that wonderful adventure with Him—through His strength, not mine.

God speaks to me personally now, but back then he spoke through a farmer named Frank. Frank died a few years back when cancer overtook him. I will never forget that wonderful man who mentored me. He loved me and gave of himself unselfishly. He gave even when I could not pay him.

Have you been mentored by someone as you travel your Christian walk? Has someone made a profound difference in your life? Has someone been a "Frank" to you? When you have been set free, be open to mentoring someone who is coming down the road behind you. Be a Frank in someone's life.

> . . . I tried keeping rules and working my head off to please God, and it didn't work. So I quit being a "law man" so that I could be God's man. Christ's life showed me how, and enabled me to do it. I identified myself completely with him. Indeed, I have been crucified with Christ. My ego is no longer central. It is no longer important that I appear righteous before you or have your good opinion, and I am no longer driven to impress God. Christ lives in me. The life you see me living is not "mine," but it is lived by faith in the Son of God, who loved me and gave himself for me . . .
>
> GALATIANS 2:20 (THE MESSAGE)

Being Honest with Myself:

Am I willing to be mentored, or is my life being developed by the Lord so that I can mentor someone else?

Inconvenienced

I n the summertime, our son Chris loved to go out to the country and play with a friend's daughter. Ed, our friend, taught at a local college in Springfield. He had written a very good book on sign language, which we were trying to teach our son. We did not know much ourselves, so Chris would go visit Ed's daughter, Starla, who would help him with his signing.

One day when I got home, I was completely exhausted. I had worked all night, and taking Chris north of town that day seemed out of the question. But how can you say no to a four-year-old kid who keeps rubbing the palm of his hand on his chest (the sign for "please")? As we started up Highway 13, I noticed a hitchhiker standing beside the road, desperately trying to get someone to stop. I felt the Lord tug on me, and I knew I was supposed to pick this guy up.

"Lord, I don't pick up hitchhikers, especially with my four-year-old son in the back seat," I said.

"John, I want you to pick up this one."

"Lord, is that your voice?" I asked.

"Yes. Pick up this man."

I turned the car around, making all the loops to get back, hoping by the time I returned, someone else would have picked him up. No such luck. There he stood. I pulled out in front of him and had enough time to ask the Lord one more time.

"Lord, are you *sure* you want me to pick this guy up?"

"John, pick him up!"

"Okay, Lord."

I asked the young man where he was headed. He said Bolivar,

which is a little town about 30 miles north of Springfield. He added that he appreciated the lift. I told him that I was not going all the way to Bolivar, but that I could take him three or four miles in the direction he needed to go. He said that would be fine. As it turned out, he was a student at Southwest Baptist University in Bolivar, his car was broken down, he was taking a summer school class, and he was trusting the Lord to provide a ride to school every day for several weeks.

"This is where I turn off," I told him. "I hope things work out for you. Blessings." I dropped him off at an intersection. I then proceeded to take Chris to Starla's. Driving back to Highway 13, I kept wondering if the young student had found a ride. Pulling up to the stop sign, I had my answer: he was standing on the side of the road, cars whizzing by.

"John, would you inconvenience yourself and take him to Bolivar?"

"Lord, that is thirty miles each way. I'm exhausted," I answered tiredly.

"I know, but I would like you to take him to Bolivar."

"Okay, Lord. Just don't let me go to sleep at the wheel."

I drove him to Bolivar; he thanked me and added that he was not late for class. I turned and headed the 30 miles back to Springfield with the windows down and the radio blaring to help me stay awake. As I got back to the north side of town, the Lord's wonderful voice entered my thoughts:

"John, would you take that young man to Bolivar everyday if I asked you to?"

I thought about that, and finally said, "Lord, if you want me to, I will."

But I never saw that young man again.

Are you willing to be inconvenienced, or are you just too busy? I wonder how many times we miss God's voice because we are simply not willing to go out of our way.

> *But a Samaritan, as he traveled, came where the man was; and when he saw him, he took pity on him.*
>
> LUKE 10:33 (NIV)

Being Honest with Myself:

Am I willing to be inconvenienced for the sake of Christ, or is this life all about me?

The Greatest Miracle
I Have Ever Seen

"Dad, can we go play golf?" my nine-year-old son signed to me.

"All right; I'll take you this afternoon, okay?" I answered.

Chris went out in the backyard to hit practice balls. Being deaf, he loved to play individual sports; team sports were never much fun for him since he was usually the only deaf person on the team. So Chris and I would go out to a par three course on the north side of Springfield right next to the interstate. We played a couple of times a week. He loved it.

The weatherman was calling for bad storms for that evening, but I thought we could get in our nine holes if we hit the links about 3:00 p.m. As we were making our way around the golf course, I started noticing the western sky toward Tulsa getting very dark. I encouraged Chris to play fast, as we were as far from the car as we could get. Within the next few minutes, we were engulfed in a monsoon. The wind was blowing cups and papers over our head; the rain was coming down in sheets. I started running for the car with my golf clubs, assuming that Chris was right behind me.

I turned to see if Chris was following me; he was not there. The rain was coming down even harder as I tried to see where he was. The sky was pitch black in every direction, but I could faintly see that he was still standing on the green. I had run about one hundred yards, and since he was deaf, I could not yell for him to come. I picked up my clubs and ran back to the green where Chris was standing. Quite frankly, I was disgusted and signed emphatically, "What are you doing?" The wind and rain had not let up one bit, and the sky was as black as coal. So there we stood, rain coming down in sheets, wind blowing so hard we could hardly stand, an ominous cloud-cover hanging over us that showed no break in any direction.

"What are you doing?" I asked again, getting more frustrated by the second. He signed back to me:

"I am going to pray to Jesus to stop the rain."

All I remember is signing: "*What?*"

Lifting his head, rain pelting his face, he signed to Heaven: "Jesus, please stop the rain so Dad and I can finish our golf game. Amen."

What happened next is the greatest miracle I have ever seen. That little guy had no sooner said "Amen" then the sky broke open, the clouds split in two, and the rain and wind ceased. Up to that time, the storm had not abated one bit. I will never forget that bright beam of light coming straight down on us on that golf green. I was soaked and in shock. Tears streamed down my face as the awesome reality of the power of God struck me.

I looked at Chris and signed, "Chris, did you just see what God did? Chris, I just saw the greatest miracle I've ever seen!"

Chris just looked at me and asked if we could finish the golf game. I was crying so hard, I tried again to explain the magnitude of what had just occurred. "Son!" I signed, "You don't understand; God just split the skies for you!"

Then the wonderful voice of God interrupted me. "*John, it is you that does not understand, oh you of little faith.*"

I looked over to where Chris was lining up a putt. I stood and watched that storm continue in two different directions. Rain was coming down just as hard as ever on both sides of the little par three course, but Chris and I were engulfed in sunshine.

> . . . *Nothing, you see, is impossible with God.*

> LUKE 1:37 (THE MESSAGE)

. . . It's impossible to please God apart from faith. And why? Because anyone who wants to approach God must believe both that he exists and that he cares enough to respond to those who seek him.

HEBREWS 11:6 (THE MESSAGE)

Being Honest with Myself:

Do I believe God; do I have faith? There is no pleasing Him without it.

Aslan

B efore he was a year old, a big black lab wandered up three floors to my friend Norm's apartment. Norm's girlfriend named the dog Aslan. Norm could not keep the dog, so I brought him home. Our lives would never be the same. I suppose everyone who has ever owned a Labrador Retriever could tell the most wonderful stories, but I want to tell you about how God used Aslan to teach me a great truth.

Against my wife's wishes, I made Aslan a house dog, even though he weighed one hundred pounds. During the day, he would stay in the backyard with only a chain link fence between him and freedom. Since he hated being alone in that backyard, he would often take off to make his routine visits around town. First, it was off to the emergency room of the hospital down the street to visit with the staff (he would use the automatic doors for easy access). Then he would go to the high school across the road for lunch at the back door of the cafeteria. Next: to K-mart to visit the warehouse crew. Finally, he would go to a local grocery store, stroll through the automatic doors to the back of the meat department, and beg for scraps.

This was not something Aslan did every once in a while; this was a weekly occurrence for years. The problem was if I tied him up, he would moan and groan; it would only work for a couple of days. Then he would be off to visit with his friends again. But he would always be home around 4:00 p.m. so we would not know he had been gone—except that is for the calls on the answering machine alerting us to his whereabouts.

One morning when I went fishing, Aslan crawled in bed with my wife. He stretched out, put his big head on my pillow, and went to sleep. You can only imagine how Brenda felt when she leaned over to hug me that Saturday morning!

On another occasion my wife cooked a fourteen-pound turkey, put it on the stove to cool, and left for the store. When she returned home, there was no turkey, no bones, no juice, only the wire that had tied the turkey legs together. Brenda heard loud moaning from the office in the back of the house. Aslan slept outside that night.

Through the years that dog ate Brenda's cakes, chickens, and other foods too numerous to mention. He dug three-foot holes in every flowerbed we ever planted. He ran off with female dogs (until our little trip to the doctor) that led to phone calls asking us if we wanted the puppies or if we wanted them to be given away. He slept by our bed and usually had gas so bad it would wake us up at night. When my wife put new carpet in the bedroom, he was moved five feet out into the hall. He always had to go out around 3:00 in the morning and never failed to come home with something from someone else's house. He hated baths, did not want to eat anything but table scraps, and he loved to ride in the car (especially at Christmas because he loved the lights). In the winter he hogged the heat by the fireplace, and in the summer he slept on the vents when the air conditioning was running.

In spite of everything, Aslan was loyal; he loved us. He did not want us to leave him and probably logged 150,000 miles in my truck. He would not let another dog within a block of our home, and all strangers were held at bay until we gave the okay; then he was off to sleep. If anyone was sick in our house, that dog wouldn't leave their side, not even to visit K-mart. Quite honestly, we loved him.

He died two weeks before he was thirteen. My wife and I cried just as hard as the children did. I buried him in the yard and thanked God for that dog. I am not sure about dogs, but I know Heaven has animals. I would love to see him again.

What does all this have to do with God? Well, one day at lunch I was sitting in my truck watching someone play with their dogs when that wonderful voice came to me. *"You know John,"* God said, *"Christians are a lot like Aslan. They dig big holes, they wander off, and they are always doing something they shouldn't . . . but I love them, I take care of them, and I train them. John, follow me. "*

Have you dug a big hole for yourself? Have you wandered off and disobeyed? Or are you at the Master's feet? If you are always breaking out and doing things that God did not plan for you, He is waiting for you to come home.

> *We all, like sheep, have gone astray, each of us has turned to his own way; and the Lord has laid on him the iniquity of us all.*
>
> ISAIAH 53:6 (NIV)

Being Honest with Myself:

Am I a wandering Christian?

Lassie

The first stop on our mission trip was Quito, Ecuador. Our destination was Riobambia, a city about one hundred miles south of Quito located high in the Andes Mountains. Our goal was to help build a Bible school for the Chichewa Indians. Approximately sixty people from our church had descended upon Riobambia. A lot of grueling labor lay ahead of us.

Now, the missionaries we met there were a wonderful couple. Our group could not have asked for better hosts, but their dog . . . well, she was another thing. The missionaries owned a German Shepherd Dog named Lassie; they assured us she was kind and gentle. She was anything but those two things. She bit two of our people and would lunge at anyone with one intent—tearing a limb off! The dog became a sore spot, but the host family assured us that they would "deal with the dog."

"John, get up and pray; it's important," I would hear the Lord say. Quietly, I would sneak out around 4:00 in the morning to pray on the roof of the school.

The first time I went up the stairs to pray, I opened the door to the roof, and that dog lunged at me, trying to tear into my leg. I kicked, and the dog backed up and attacked again. I lashed out with my shoe while the dog circled, waiting for an opportunity to sink its teeth into me. I threw open the outside door with a flourish, scaring the dog far enough away so I could walk out on the top of the roof. The roof was several thousand square feet. I found a corner and looked back to where the dog was circling by the door. She was like a wolf waiting for the right moment to pounce. This standoff went on for almost twenty minutes, until finally I said, "Lord, I can't pray; I'm scared of this dog." The Lord did not say anything back, but I will never forget what happened next.

That dog melted like butter. She put her head down, walked right up to me, and rubbed her side against my leg. She was perfectly calm and gentle. I reached down, and she let me stroke her side. As I walked for two hours praying on the roof, Lassie walked with me. Never again did she show any aggression toward me. In fact, I would take food scraps from supper the night before, and she would eat right out of my hand.

Other people on the team were not so fortunate, and after about four days, Lassie's owners moved her early each morning to another location where she could not hurt anyone. But every night she was put on the roof again, where she walked beside me like a faithful friend.

> *The Lord who delivered me from the paw of the lion and the paw of the bear will deliver me from the hand of this Philistine . . .*
>
> 1 SAMUEL 17:37 (NIV)

> *Even though I walk through the valley of the shadow of death, I will fear no evil, for you are with me; your rod and your staff, they comfort me.*
>
> PSALM 23:4 (NIV)

Being Honest with Myself:

What do I fear that keeps me from growing closer to God?

My Greatest Week of Prayer

God first impacted me in regard to prayer in 1988. Up to that time I did not take prayer seriously. Now mind you, it was not that I thought it was unimportant or that it would not work. It is just that up until that time, I think I prayed mostly selfish prayers, prayers that probably made God say something like, *"You've got a lot to learn, son."* Since 1988, I have been on a prayer journey, an adventure that I can only attribute to grace and obedience. I wish I could tell you I have never missed a day of prayer the last sixteen years, but that would be wrong. I have struggled through dry times, sometimes months where Heaven seemed closed. I have had issues in my life that God has pointed out that I did not make right with Him, and if we regard wickedness in our hearts, God will not hear us until we repent. I have been tired, other times sick; but still by grace, God has allowed me to minister to Him. I have spent thousands of hours with Him in the last sixteen years, and I can tell you that there is nothing on earth we can experience that is compared with being in His presence. I would rather die than miss Him. He rewards those that diligently seek Him; He gives grace to each person to seek Him, and the reward is God Himself. But since mission work is exhausting and it is often difficult to wake up to pray, when I arrived in Ecuador in the Andes Mountains, I told God that He would have to give me the strength to pray. Little did I know that this would be the greatest week of prayer I would ever experience.

I first sensed God speaking to me as we traveled from Quito to Riobambia, a distance of 125 miles through the Andes Mountains. He spoke very quietly at first; His voice began as a quiet impression, but within 24 hours that impression grew much stronger as God called me to intercede for Ecuador. As God shared His heart with me that afternoon and into the night, I knew He wanted me to pray, to storm Heaven for Ecuador, especially the indigenous people: the Chichewa Indians. These Indians are the descendents of the Incas. Until the 1960s, these people were not even recognized as legitimate human beings; in their country they were considered lower than dogs.

As I walked out on the roof that first morning, the Lord said to me: *"John, I will anoint you to pray, to stand in the gap, to fight the forces of hell that keep this country in bondage. I will stay with you until the first person comes on the roof; then you will know it is over and you can leave."* He wanted me to call and wait for His power to come as a fire from Heaven. I cannot ever remember weeping so hard or feeling His burden as heavily as I did that week.

Each morning, the Lord would wake me between 4:00 and 4:30 in the morning. Without fail, He would come in power as I interceded for these people who needed Jesus. Usually around seven o'clock, someone from the team would come up to view the beautiful mountains that surrounded the city and the volcano located about thirty miles away that was spewing lava and ash. I would hear that wonderful voice say, *"John, I will meet you here in the morning, and I will walk with you all day."*

One morning I awoke at 3:00 in the morning. I said, "Lord, you are a little early today."

"Yes, I am. I need you to get up. It's important," He replied.

I lay there thinking about it, trying to get my bearings, when I heard that wonderful voice speak again: *"John, it is very important today. Come be with me."*

As I found my way to the roof, something seemed different. I can only say that there was un-holiness in the atmosphere, an eerie feeling of demonic activity. This might sound strange to some people, but these things, of course, are spiritually discerned. We need to recognize that "we do not wrestle against flesh and blood, but against principalities, against powers, against the rulers of the darkness of this age, against spiritual hosts of wickedness in the heavenly places," Ephesians 6:12 (NKJV).

I worshipped the great God and Savior for about two hours that day, but the time passed quickly, as if I had only prayed for two minutes. His Spirit flooded my soul as I lifted my hands to Him and put my face on the ash-covered roof. Finally, power came to me to pray down principalities and powers. I knew they had been brought low before Him in whose presence they tremble. James 2:19 (NIV) says "You believe that there is one God. Good! Even the demons believe that—and shudder." God had specifically told me to pray against the evil that controlled and corrupted this region, and at the end of the week on Halloween, God impressed upon me that He had broken strongholds in the spiritual realm. At about 6:00 in the morning, I asked the Lord what had been going on. He simply said:

"John, today is Halloween, and much evil has gone out on the earth."

A word of instruction here: God did not give me all the specifics, and I did not ask, but He uses prayer to bring evil low, accomplish His will, and advance His kingdom throughout the earth.

I never followed up with anything specific, but I know from one report I heard that God is moving mightily among this people once considered lower than dogs. Small villages throughout the Andes are being changed by the gospel of Jesus Christ. God is raising people up to pray. If He is calling you to pray for someone today, whether it is the Chichewa Indians or your next door neighbor, obey Him. You could make a difference to someone He loves dearly.

> *I looked for someone to stand up for me against all this, to repair the defenses of the city, to take a stand for me and stand in the gap to protect this land so I wouldn't have to destroy it. I couldn't find anyone. Not one.*
>
> EZEKIEL 22:30 (THE MESSAGE)

> *Here's what I want you to do: Find a quiet, secluded place so you won't be tempted to role-play before God. Just be there as simply and honestly as you can manage. The focus will shift from you to God, and you will begin to sense his grace.*
>
> MATTHEW 6:6 (THE MESSAGE)

Being Honest with Myself:

Is God important enough to me that I would seek Him in prayer, or are my prayers all about me?

A Girl Named Dalexia

n March of 1999, I took a trip with our church to Honduras, a small country in Latin America. The country had been devastated by a hurricane; the whole country looked as though it had floated away. Huge sections of road were gone. Houses were wiped out by the thousands; rivers had formed where previously there was no water at all. The people were displaced into makeshift shelters made from anything they could get their hands on—tin, plastic, cardboard, and old tires were stacked and formed as temporary homes.

We were to live for five days in a village called El Estrebo. This village is located about a half mile from Nicaragua and ten miles or so from the Pacific Ocean. To get there, we took the Pan American highway, drove about five miles on a dirt road, and finally reached the village. In the village, you could see the devastation of the hurricane. All the buildings that were constructed using handmade mud bricks were gone; the hurricane had disintegrated them. The only buildings left were bamboo huts and a few concrete buildings the government had built. While there was destruction everywhere, our time there was to be spent specifically rebuilding a church and parsonage.

We set up tents that would be our home for the next five days. My friend Dan and I had the job of making sure everyone had three meals a day, the camp was clean, and none of our supplies were stolen, since thievery was prevalent there. Most of the people in the village had never ventured out of El Estrebo, so when about twenty *gringos* showed up with all kinds of food and interesting gadgets, it caused quite a stir. The bathhouse (that had no door or roof) and toilet (that also had no door) were located right next to our camp.

Our camp became a busy place as curious onlookers congregated to see what the Americans were up to and to receive a treat or two. I had brought a suitcase full of toys, coloring books, balls, crayons, Kool-Aid, Gator-Aid, and candy to give away. So "Juan" (that's me) became the man to see in El Estrebo. Dozens of women and children and a few men came to check out the situation. One group of children in particular came to see me often: a group of six little girls, all around nine years old. In that group was a small girl named Dalexia, a girl who would forever change my life.

As those girls walked into the camp for the first time, my eye immediately focused on her. She had no shoes and wore a ragged blue dress. Though frail-looking, she was solid from carrying water and performing the demanding physical labor that is required of the children in her country. Something very strange happened when I lay eyes on this little girl. I immediately fell in love with her, as a father would love his most precious daughter. For the next two days, I literally ached for this child. I could not wait until she and her friends got out of school and could come see me. I was constantly trying to think of some way I could get her back to the United States so she could have all the wonderful advantages that my children had.

Although there were often more than fifty children running around, I found myself treating Dalexia with special care. On the third evening, however, all the children came to get candy and drinks except Dalexia. I was devastated. In broken Spanish, I asked where she was. She could not come tonight, they said. *Why?* I thought. *Have I done something wrong?* My heart was broken. I wondered if I would ever see her again. That whole evening I was troubled by my feelings for this child; they were not improper, but they were intense—as intense as my love for my wife when we first met. I can tell you that the ache to rescue this child and save her from the terrible life she was forced to live was as deep as I have ever had for a human being. My feelings were magnified even more as she had not shown up that evening.

I went about my duties and cleaned up the camp with my friend Dan, then went to lie down on my sleeping bag in the tent. The wind was blowing briskly that night, and the sky was full of stars. I lay down and said, "God, what are these feelings I have for this child? I have been in other countries, and I have seen the poor and homeless, but I have never felt this way."

The Lord said this to me: *"John, I have put in you the intense love you have for this child. That is My heart. John, you were that little child, without hope. I looked down the path of time and saw you coming, and I wanted you and said I would take care of you. I wanted to adopt you into my family and love you forever,"* God told me. *"When Dalexia did not come tonight and your heart was broken, John, that is how I feel when you don't come, when you don't have time for me. John, you are special to me, and now you know how I feel about you."*

I cried myself to sleep that night. I do not know if my tent mates Bill or John knew what was going on, but that night, a 47-year-old man never felt more loved by his Abba Father.

I knew I would probably never again visit El Estrabo or see the beautiful little Honduran girl. Through an interpreter I told Dalexia the story of Jesus. She assured me that she knew Him and would see me in Heaven. When our five days were complete, we loaded the vehicles and drove away. As we drove back to the capital of Honduras, my feelings for that child had not subsided. I lay down on the bed at the hotel and cried, "Lord, I can't live this way. I can't, Lord."

He said to me, *"I know, John. But you will never forget how I love you."*

"No, Lord, I won't forget."

The feelings left, and I took a nap.

We love because he first loved us.

1 JOHN 4:19 (NIV)

. . . He predestined us to be adopted as his sons through Jesus Christ, in accordance with his pleasure and will . . .

EPHESIANS 1:5 (NIV)

> *But God demonstrates His own love toward us, in that while we*
> *were still sinners, Christ died for us.*

ROMANS 5:8 (NKJV)

Being Honest with Myself:

Do I really believe God loves me unconditionally, or have I forgotten the cross?

Does God Heal?

ealing is an attention-grabbing subject. Whole denominations and movements have been started because of it; other
denominations and movements have downplayed healing
to the point of ignoring the subject. I grew up in the latter movement.
In 1986, God taught me a valuable lesson about healing, one that I
will never forget.

In 1984 a true movement of God started at a church that I attended in Springfield, Missouri. People were flocking to this particular church; they would stand outside the windows and in the hallways
in the summer to listen to the pastor. This movement was probably
the closest thing to revival I have ever experienced. Things were happening so fast that it was difficult to keep up with what was going on
in the church.

The move of God began when our pastor attended a James
Robinson conference in Dallas and came back with a new enthusiasm
for the Word of God—and a renewed passion for revival. From time
to time, speakers would come that had knowledge regarding issues
related to this particular Baptist church. One specific speaker from
Florida came to conduct a three or four day meeting. That Sunday
night, I was sitting on the third row about eight feet from the stage. At
some point the speaker stopped and said that God had told him there
were six people that would be healed that night of blood problems.
Now, I don't care to get graphic, but let's just say that when I went to
the bathroom, it showed up. I had been too embarrassed to say anything, even to my wife, but it was becoming a problem.

When this man spoke, the Lord said to me: *"John, you are one of those six people, and if you will step out in faith, I will heal you."* I had only eight feet to walk. When the preacher put a small amount of oil on my head, I knew I was healed.

That was eighteen years ago—and I am still healed. Now to answer the question I proposed: does God heal? No doubt about it. How do you explain it? Well, I am not prepared to make a lengthy dissertation on healing; this is just the story of what I experienced. But I will let you in on a little secret. Psalms 115:3 says " . . . for our God is in heaven; He does whatever He pleases" (NKJV).

Bottom line: God is sovereign. Period.

I hate to end this story because I know some people will ask, "What about this?" or "What about that?" I'll leave that discussion for another book. The point is our Great God does things for His glory. If you are sick, you should call upon the name of the Lord, for He is a God of compassion and mercy (Psalm 86:15).

> *Praise the Lord, O my soul, and forget not all his benefits—who forgives all your sins and heals all your diseases, who redeems your life from the pit and crowns you with love and compassion, who satisfies your desires with good things so that your youth is renewed like the eagle's.*
>
> PSALM 103:2–5 (NIV)

Being Honest with Myself:

Do I seek the Lord first for problems, or is He just another stop on my list of places to turn?

AIDS and Brother Bill

William Richard Gordon was the name my parents gave my little brother when he entered the world in 1959. "Bill," as we called him, was seven years younger than me. I cannot say I remember much about him until he got older. He spent his senior year in high school living with my wife and me. After graduation, he headed off to Charlotte, North Carolina, to manage a restaurant.

Now the one thing about my brother that was evident from the start was that God made him good-looking. My mother used to say that he was better looking than a Greek god. While in Charlotte he met a beautiful girl, and they began to pursue modeling careers together. Both of them quickly took off in the profession, so they quit their jobs and moved to the Big Apple.

The next several years were good to them in terms of work. They both made it to the big time and became professional models. It is kind of odd to see your little brother on game boxes, billboards, magazines, and Calvin Klein commercials. He was well-known and made a decent wage. However, as is often the case, fame and fortune came at a high price.

The phone rang one day, and my wife answered. I could tell the news was not good.

"What's wrong?" I whispered in the background. She looked incredibly sad.

She hung up the phone and just looked at me. Finally, she said, "Bill has AIDS. It's not good."

"I should go see him," I answered immediately. "Book me a ticket for October."

We had known about his homosexual lifestyle for several years. As Christians, we did not approve, but we loved him. My wife had been especially gentle and kind to Bill, and he loved her very much. I, on the other hand, had taken a more macho approach. God had dealt with me over this several years earlier, yet the residue still lingered. I loved Bill, but I was disgusted, hurt, and did not know how to deal with it.

On the way to New York City, all I kept thinking was, *God, how do I deal with this?*

The Lord would say, "*John, you can't. I will live through you.*"

I had never been to New York, but I was about to learn what Dorothy learned: that I was not in "Kansas" anymore. I found a brownstone where I could stay that was close to where John Lennon was shot, a halfway house for missionaries returning from overseas. Under the circumstances, they would let me stay there for a donation of $20 a day. The cabby dropped me off, and I made plans to get to the hospital located near the Empire State Building. I quickly learned that busses and subways were the way to go or else I had to walk. I did a lot of walking that week.

When I got to the hospital, the staff told me that Bill was on the AIDS floor. I walked in and was informed by three nurses that I had to wear a mask due to a tuberculosis alert on that particular day. I went through the double doors and down the hall, past people who had no hope of survival. They were moaning and screaming. I heard their cries all the way to my brother's room. Before I opened the door, I made one last plea to God to help me get through this situation. I felt sudden peace take hold of me as I opened the door. Bill was sitting up in bed; he had not been awake for long.

"Hey, buddy," I said, "I brought that cashew chicken from Springfield that you like." I helped him set up the food, taking his rolling tray and unloading the food on it. "This should be good. I got it just before I left," I told him.

"Thanks, John," he answered quietly. "I've been looking forward to this."

It was all I could do not to cry. The once good-looking model who had been voted one of the top 25 best-looking models in America—my brother—sat there stooped over, his hair falling out, his six foot plus body carrying no more than one hundred pounds. He looked terrible.

"I appreciate your coming, John," he said to me.

"Oh, that's okay, Bill. I just wanted to see you and tell you I love you."

"I kinda blew it, didn't I?" he said quietly, looking up at me.

"Yes," I answered truthfully, "but we all do. That's why God had to send Jesus."

We sat there for several hours until he got tired. He spoke up and said, "John, I sleep a lot, and you have never seen New York City. I want you to promise me you'll go see the city."

"Bill," I said, "I didn't come here to see the city; I came here to see you!"

"I know. But promise me. It would mean something to me."

With that, I tucked him in, hugged him, and started to leave. He was dozing off when he said, "Tomorrow you will have to meet my friends."

"Okay, Bill. Get some sleep," I said. "I'll see you in the morning."

When I stepped back out into the busy streets of New York, I was crying.

The next day I met Bill's friends. I have to admit that with Bill, his friends, and his roommate, I felt a little odd; I was the only straight guy in the room. But I would hear that wonderful voice say, *"John, let Me shine through you."* And God, being true to His word, did. In fact, when I prepared to leave that night, Bill's friends thanked me for not being caustic. When I told them that Jesus loved them, they did not say much.

Bill and I had some good talks that week. One visit I remember quite well—an afternoon when I asked him, "Bill, how did you get into this lifestyle? We had the same mama; she taught us the same values." He explained, and I cried. He told me how he was coerced into the gay lifestyle, how like quicksand there was no escape. It broke my heart to hear it.

When the week was over, I went home. That was the last time I saw my brother alive. He died the following June, one week after his thirty-second birthday.

Do I believe homosexuality is the "ultimate" sin? Absolutely not. Sin is sin, and God sent Jesus who paid for the sin of the whole world. Romans 3:23 says, "for all have sinned and fall short of the glory of God" (NIV). The Bible says sin brings forth death when it has conceived. All I can say is that the world needs Christ, everyone from the elder in the church to the prostitute hustling the streets. Jesus is the answer for the world. Jesus is the one who breaks our every bondage and is willing to free the homosexual or anyone else held in bondage.

> The Spirit of the Lord God is upon me because the Lord has anointed me to preach good tidings to the poor. He has sent me to heal the brokenhearted to proclaim liberty to the captives and the opening of the prison to those who are bound . . .
>
> ISAIAH 61:1 (NKJV)

> But you, O Lord, are a compassionate and gracious God, slow to anger, abounding in love and faithfulness. Turn to me and have mercy on me; grant your strength to your servant . . .
>
> PSALM 86:15–16 (NIV)

Being Honest with Myself:

Do I have compassion, or when I view the suffering, do I judge them with disgust as not being worth the love of Christ?

The Con Man

My fourteenth and fifteenth years of life were spent in a small town in South Carolina called Travelers Rest. I remember the town's population consisted of either the extremely wealthy, who worked in Greenville, or the extremely poor, the textile workers. There was no "middle class." I had taken a job at a textile factory to help supplement our income at home. I was only fifteen, and the burden was beginning to be more than I could carry.

At that time, I met a man named Bill. Bill was about 35 years old when I first met him. He was one of those people to whom others would gravitate. Bill was handsome, quick-witted, and fun to be around. You could not help but notice him in his Hicky-Freeman suits, driving a convertible Cadillac. I met him because his mother lived down the hill from us. She had a blue and gold Macaw that Bill had given her. The bird sat outside on nice days, and I would go to her house to hear the bird talk. She would also allow me to feed it.

Bill was nice to me at a time when I had no friends. He gave our family a German Shepherd Dog that we named Buford. He would take me to get hamburgers. The summer of 1968 rolled around, and I was tired of working second shift at the factory. So when Bill offered me a job in Charlotte, North Carolina, I jumped at the opportunity. I packed what few clothes I had and headed up I-85 with Bill in his convertible Cadillac, happy to be with my new friend. That was the beginning of a summer I will not soon forget.

We pulled up to a palatial home in Charlotte, and Bill said, "Grab your things; this is where you're staying for the summer." I did not know who owned the home. I just assumed it belonged to Bill. As it turned out, a wealthy single dentist owned the home, and he and Bill lived there together. I did not have a bedroom; I slept all summer in a sitting room on a sofa. Later I learned that the home was really a party house with prostitutes coming and going three or four nights a week. All kinds of shady characters showed up, most of whom never spoke to me except to say, "Who's the kid?" Someone would always answer, "He's okay; he's with Bill."

My job was to care for all the fish, reptiles, and animals he kept in a pet wholesale warehouse. The warehouse was located in an old building in a very bad part of Charlotte. Bill had given me about one week of training for the job, and he had hired one other kid to help with deliveries. The other kid was gone all the time in the van making the rounds, so I was alone most of the time.

I thought it was kind of fun taking care of the animals, especially since Bill didn't sell two of the animals but let me keep them all summer long. One was a spider monkey that I named Simon. The other was a Cockatoo from Australia that I named Sam. I would let Simon and Sam out of their cages, and they would hang around me until the lights went out at night.

I remember one day, Bill left a wallet on his desk. I was caught up on all my duties, so I decided to take a peek. In the wallet were sixteen driver's licenses from sixteen different states. *That's odd*, I thought. The seeds of suspicion were planted in the back of my mind. I began to notice other things. I had been given specific instructions on how to answer the phone—most specifically, Bill's name was not to be mentioned. As the weeks passed, I started to realize through different events that Bill was a first-class con man, a "grifter."

Bill was always kind to me, and while he did not shower me with money, he took me to lavish places. Though I was beginning to see the side of him that most people never knew about, I looked the other way and pretended not to see because he was living the good life, and I was living some of it with him.

Once I was waiting for Bill in his car outside a bank. The Cadillac's top was down, and it was a pretty day. I thought, *I want to be like Bill when I grow up*. Bill came walking out of the bank with a roll of cash that could choke a horse, threw me a $20, and said "Nice day, John. Nice day, don't you think?"

I turned to Bill and said, "You know, Bill, I'd like to be like you when I grow up."

He just looked at me; he never said a word.

About six years later, I was married and living in Springfield, Missouri, when I received a phone call from my mother.

"John," she said, "I'm just calling to let you know that Bill has died."

I asked her how. She said he had died of lung cancer. Bill had been a chain smoker, which was cool in the sixties.

My mother continued: "John, his mother said he wanted to tell you one thing before he died."

I asked what it was, and she relayed Bill's last message to me:

"Tell John not to become like me."

The Lord nudged me when I heard that and said: *"John, I want you to be like Me."*

You know, we live in a world where everyone wants to look like a movie star, be a famous jock, or become powerful or rich like a well-known politician or businessman. I want to challenge you to be thankful and grateful for the way God made you. Realize He has a wonderful plan for your life. God has called all of us to be conformed to His image. Do not listen to the world and all the voices that tell you to "look like that" or "act like this." That is just a con job.

> *Do not be misled: "Bad company corrupts good character."*
>
> 1 CORINTHIANS 15:33 (NIV)

Being Honest with Myself:

Is it my goal to be like others . . . or like Jesus?

Not Today

Ever since I was young, I have always enjoyed hunting and fishing. It is not something I get to do all the time, but even as an adult when I go bass fishing or hunting with a couple of buddies, I sure enjoy it.

In 1973, I took up bow-hunting for white-tailed deer. My friend Rex and I always looked forward to October 1, which is the opening day for bow season in Missouri. Early fall in the Ozarks is beautiful; the leaves are turning and the air is crisp. When October rolled around, I could not wait to climb up in that deer stand in the peace and quiet of the Ozark woods. My father-in-law had several hundred acres in the Branson area, so Rex and I mainly hunted there.

Rex and I had made plans to go hunting one October evening, but Rex called and told me he could not go. I had been looking forward to it, so I decided to go alone. The drive from Springfield to Branson is about forty miles. In 1973, the highway was two-lanes with a seventy mile per hour speed limit. I finished hunting and started to head home in my Mercury Capri. I was very, very tired that night, but I knew it was only forty miles, and then I would be home.

When I was about fifteen miles north of Branson, I fell asleep. I awoke suddenly when I felt my steering wheel wrenched from my hands, as though an unseen hand had taken control. I was no longer driving my four-speed car. I was still trying to figure out what was happening around me, because I could hear horns honking and lights were blinding my eyes. As I was headed down the hill toward Busiek Forest, my car was moving at over eighty miles per hour approaching the bottom of the hill. My car crossed over the lane into the oncoming traffic and passed over the shoulder and down into the ditch. My car was driven out of the ditch, across the road, to the shoulder, and parked—all while I was still trying to get my bearings. I sat there while cars that were parked on the bridge filed past. The cars had stopped to watch me crash and to avoid being hit by me as I crossed back over into their lane. As I sat there in that little car trying to focus and think about what had happened, I started to shake.

At that moment, the distinct voice of God said, *"John, I am not finished with your life yet."*

I have thought many times about that night when God saved my life and told me "not today." I once heard a missionary say, "We are indestructible until God is finished with our lives." How true that is. Nothing can harm you, nothing, until the Father says, "Today."

> *You have decided the length of our lives. You know how many months we will live, and we are not given a minute longer.*
>
> JOB 14:5 (NLT)

> *. . . man is destined to die once, and after that to face judgment . . .*
>
> HEBREWS 9:27 (NIV)

Being Honest with Myself:

Do I believe God has a purpose for my life, or do I just drift?

Go Buy Stamps

n April of 1984, my daughter was barely two years old, and we needed some things from the store. By the time I headed to Dillon's Grocery store on South Campbell in Springfield to pick up the items my wife had requested, it was already dark. Very few cars were parked in the parking lot, so I got a space right in front of the door. I grabbed a cart and headed down the aisle to collect the things on the list.

The country radio station was playing in the store, and they were reporting ominous-looking storms that had moved into our area. Storm watchers had seen funnel clouds in and around Republic, a town about twelve miles west of Springfield. The radio announcers were going crazy trying to keep up with the reports.

I got my items and headed for the checkout to pay my bill and get back home. I made it as far as the automatic doors when the Lord spoke to me: *"John, go buy stamps."*

I thought I had not heard right. Finally I said, "Lord, it is late on Friday night; I don't need stamps."

Again, He said to me: *"John, go buy stamps, and buy them now."*

"Okay, Lord," I answered.

Leaving my basket by the doors, I headed over to the service counter, pulled out a dollar bill, and asked the lady for a dollar's worth of stamps.

"I'll need to change out this cash drawer first; give me a couple of minutes. I'll be right back," she said.

I stood there until she got back, handed her the money, put the stamps in my pocket, and headed for the front door to retrieve my cart and drive home. I had just put my hands on the cart handle and started to push it out the door when one of the grocery handlers came running into the store, yelling, "There's a tornado across the street!" That caught everyone's attention, but no sooner did the young man yell "tornado" than the power went out. The store was pitch black. As my eyes adjusted, I finally saw that a few emergency lights were working.

Someone yelled, "There's a basement in the back of the stock room—run!" I started running down the aisle and almost tripped over a mother and her daughter who were huddled on the floor, clutching one another and crying. Just as I stopped, I heard the crashing of glass blowing out of the front windows. I put my arms around the lady and girl and said, "You have to come with me." We ran to the back of the store, but we never made it to the basement. I crouched down by some cereal boxes, wrapped my arms around the two women, and pleaded, "Lord, I need you now." Then the Lord spoke these words to me:

"John, because you are in this store, no one will be hurt."

Whether I was the only Christian in the store that night I do not know, but God showed me favor, and every person in the store along with me. If you saw the movie *Twister*, that is what the next few minutes were like. The sound was just like a locomotive. I could hear glass breaking. The building seemed to be heaving. Large parts of the grocery shelving were being tossed about; items from the shelves were thrown through the air. Lights were blowing up. Water was pouring through the store. I put my body over the two women's backs and tried to comfort them, saying, "The Lord told me we will be okay." They continued to cry.

When the storm finally passed, I jumped up to see if everyone had made it to the back. I walked out the swinging doors but could not see anything. Food and grocery items were a foot deep down the aisles. I waded through the mess up to the flashlights, stuffing batteries into them quickly. By the time I had about three flashlights ready, people were finding their way to the front of the store. I handed the flashlights out and told three employees to make sure no one was caught in the aisles. When they took off to hunt for people, the Lord spoke to me again:

"John, they are okay."

I got to thinking about my wife and kids, wondering if they were okay. There was no glass left in the windows, so I jumped through toward my car. When I saw my car, I realized it was totally destroyed. The glass had imploded, and there was a board that had come through the back glass and lodged itself between the front and back seats—right where my head would have been. I looked around the parking lot; devastation was everywhere. Three guys were taking advantage of the situation and filling up the back of their truck with cases of alcohol from what was once the liquor department of the store. Light poles and power lines were down, so I had to jump over them to get to the street. People were driving slowly by to gawk at the damage. I stopped the first car I could find; it was a couple on a date.

"Take me home," I said.

"Yeah, sure," said the guy, "you okay, man?"

At home, everything was fine. But the tornado had been the worst in the history of Springfield. Over eight hundred homes were destroyed or severely damaged. Multiple businesses were gone, and several people died. The National Guard was called out, and it took months for the city to rebuild what a storm destroyed in a matter of minutes. Having seen firsthand the power of nature that night, I can only say it makes me empathetic to those who find themselves suffering because of various forces of nature.

Every day the Lord watches over you. Think about it—every day! And if He asks you to go buy stamps, you know He has a reason—so go do it!

> *The Lord is slow to anger and great in power; the Lord will not leave the guilty unpunished. His way is in the whirlwind and the storm, and clouds are the dust of his feet.*
>
> Nahum 1:3 (NIV)

Man's days are determined; you have decreed the number of his months and have set limits he cannot exceed.

JOB 14:5 (NIV)

Being Honest with Myself:

Do I put my trust in the Lord above everything else?

A Fast from Good Works

n March of 2002, a group of men from my church took a mission trip to San Fernando de Atabapo in Venezuela. This village is located two hundred miles from the nearest road and is just across the river from Columbia, South America in Southwest Venezuela. This was my second trip to Atabapo. I was to help build a school to train locals so they could minister more effectively to the thousands of Indian villages that dot the Venezuela jungle, an area about the size of Mississippi. Without going into specific detail, the demonic is prevalent in that region of the world. Demons are very active in the Venezuelan Amazon. More on this subject can be read in the book *Spirit of the Rainforest*, which chronicles an influential *shaman*, or witchdoctor, who was subsequently saved and told his story to a missionary. Every village has *shamen*. The village of Atabapo is likewise deluged with *shamen*, and the people experience many problems with homosexuality, prostitution, and more. Much prayer is needed to bring revival to this region.

On the third morning, I was awakened by the Spirit of the Lord at 4:00 a.m. with a strong mandate to pray for Bob and Lisa Holloway's ministry and the work there in the jungle. Not wanting to wake my traveling companions, I decided to slip down to the missionary's house and pray under a palm branch-covered pavilion. I leaned a chair up against a post, turned on my praise CD, and proceeded to worship and praise my friend and Savior, Jesus. About two hours went by, and I was still simply worshipping the High One; I could not stop praising Him, which was fine with me. I enjoyed the strong anointing to exalt the Most High and lift Him up where evil is so prevalent.

At about 6:30 in the morning, the sun began to come up over the jungle canopy. I was facing the east, admiring the beautiful sunrise and listening to worship music when the Lord spoke these words to me:

"John, I am going to pour out My Spirit on this village. I want you to gather items to give to these people, to bless them and Bob and Lisa." Then the Lord reminded me of a Scripture, Romans 2:4, stating that the goodness and kindness of the Lord leads to repentance.

I didn't hear anything more than that, but God put in me an insatiable desire to help Bob, Lisa, and the people to whom they had been sent to preach the gospel. I came home from that trip with a passion to purchase items, raise money, solicit gifts—in short, to do whatever had to be done to fulfill the mandate the Great One had given me. I set out to fill a cargo shipping container. I had about sixteen to eighteen months to complete this mission. It was a good work indeed.

I had diligently worked at this project for about eight months, and God was greatly blessing my efforts. But in November of 2002, I sensed dryness in my soul. Looking back, it had been slowly coming on me for several months, but I had been so obsessed with reaching the challenge God had set before me, I really had not paid very close attention to it. My relationship with Jesus had suffered. One morning I was praying, and I commented to the Lord that I did not sense His presence that well. He answered:

"John, I see the good work you are doing to help the people in Venezuela, but that work has become more important to you than I am. You've let that work replace our relationship." He reminded me of Revelation 2:2–4, which says:

> *I know your deeds, your hard work and your perseverance. I know*
> *that you cannot tolerate wicked men, that you have tested those*
> *who claim to be apostles but are not, and have found them false.*
> *You have persevered and have endured hardships for my name*
> *and have not grown weary. Yet I hold this against you: You have*
> *forsaken your first love (NIV).*

When I realized my error, I wept. The Lord had one more thing to say to me about the matter, and it was a new challenge:

"John, I want you to fast forty days from buying anything for Atabapo."

I spent that time renewing my love for the Father and His Son Jesus. Much like a marriage where the couple needs to get away for a weekend and renew their love, that is how that forty days went. I experienced a love renewal for Jesus. The fast ended January 2, 2003, but I have not forgotten where my priorities should lie since then. Let me reassure you that there is nothing, not even good works that advance the kingdom, that is worth putting before Him. In a world where relationships are so flimsy, aren't you glad Jesus guards yours and mine with all diligence? Oh, what love.

> *Jesus replied, "Love the Lord with all your heart and with all your soul and with all your mind." This is the first and greatest commandment.*

> MATTHEW 22:37–38 (NIV)

Being Honest with Myself:

What good work is consuming me; has something stolen my relationship with Christ?

Flowers for a Girl

This story is about a girl whom I will call Amber. Amber is a beautiful girl, intelligent, with a vivacious personality. She is a young lady that stands out in any crowd. Her parents, too, are wonderful Christian people who are as nice to be around as anyone. However, being raised in a Christian home is no guarantee that people are immune to making mistakes.

Amber started dating a young man who was dealing drugs. One thing led to another, and she ended up hooked on this guy, "fell in love" with him, and married him without her parents' knowledge. Things got worse; this shady fellow began to abuse this wonderful girl. With her parents' help, she managed to get loose and eventually divorced him. The whole experience turned Amber back to the Lord, and she began dating a wonderful young man who treated her like a queen. They eventually became engaged. Wanting to do things right this time, she made plans to get married in a nice service with a pastor officiating. First, Amber contacted an old pastor and put in a request for him to perform the ceremony. He not only declined but was rude to her about it. She went through several clergy before finding one who agreed to oversee the wedding. Most of the pastors she contacted made it clear they would not perform the service because of her bruised past.

Now it is not my intention to debate the issue of divorce, but it is my intention to tell you about what Jesus told me when I heard of Amber's predicament. I became involved in the situation at the tail end of it, as Amber was struggling greatly with guilt and rejection from the pastors around her. When I heard about her situation, I decided to make it a focus in my prayers the next morning.

Getting up around 4:30 in the morning on a beautiful Sunday morning, I headed out in my truck to pray to my Friend who sits enthroned in Heaven.

"Good morning, John!"

"Good morning, Lord," I answered.

"John, there is something I want you to do today for me," the Lord said. *"When you are finished praying, I want you to go to the store, buy some beautiful flowers for Amber, take them to the church this morning, and leave them at the reception desk in the lobby."* He had further directions for me: *"And John, this is what I want you to put on the card"*:

> *Amber, I love you, and when you confess your sins, I am faithful*
> *and just to forgive and to cleanse, and I put them behind me.*
> *They are as far as the east is from the west. I don't remember them*
> *anymore, and you don't need to, either. You are free.*
>
> JESUS.

I did as the Lord told me, then called Amber and told her there was something for her at the reception desk.

Walking out of church later with my wife, I heard someone yell my name. I turned, and there was Amber and her mother. She came up and hugged me, tears in her eyes. God had released her.

Amber married that young man. They are as happy as any two people could be, and God is blessing them.

John 8:3–11 tells this story:

> *The teachers of the law and the Pharisees brought in a woman*
> *caught in adultery. They made her stand before the group and said*
> *to Jesus, "Teacher, this woman was caught in the act of adultery. In*
> *the Law Moses commanded us to stone such women. Now what do*
> *you say?" They were using this question as a trap, in order to have*
> *a basis for accusing him.*
>
> *But Jesus bent down and started to write on the ground with his*
> *finger. When they kept on questioning him, he straightened up and*
> *said to them, "If any one of you is without sin, let him be the first*

to throw a stone at her." Again he stooped down and wrote on the ground.

At this, those who heard began to go away one at a time, the older ones first, until only Jesus was left, with the woman still standing there. Jesus straightened up and asked her, "Woman, where are they? Has no one condemned you?"

"No one, sir," she said.

"Then neither do I condemn you," Jesus declared, "Go now and leave your life of sin" (NIV).

If you are like this woman, if you have sinned and made a bad mistake and the devil or misguided people will not let you forget it, stop beating yourself up. Confess your sin to Jesus, repent, make a 180 degree turn, and sin no more. Oh—and have a wonderful life with Christ!

"Come now, and let us reason together," says the Lord. "Though your sins are like scarlet, they shall be as white as snow; though they are red like crimson, they shall be as wool."

ISAIAH 1:18 (NKJV)

Being Honest with Myself:

How do I view people who blow it: with empathy or contempt?

A Great Grandpa

f there is one thing that none of us has control over, it is what families we are born into. However, even though our heritage is set, what we do with our spiritual lives determines what happens to future generations.

Let me give you an example: in Cape Cod, Massachusetts is a statue of pilgrim Robert Cushman. My wife is a direct descendant of this pilgrim who helped purchase the Speedwell and who reportedly preached the first sermon in America. Her family has enjoyed great blessings for generations because of this man who set the spiritual standard. A rich history.

Another note: three or four years ago, I was working for a retired pastor from Minnesota whose last name was Mather. When I made mention of the fact that I had read in *The Light and the Glory*, a book by Peter Marshall about an original pilgrim and Christian named Cotton Mather, the pastor smiled and said, "That was my grandfather. He was the first president of Harvard University and was friends with my wife's grandfather almost four hundred years ago." Small world.

My heritage is not that illustrious on my father's side. The Gordons are Scottish, probably the third largest clan in that country. If you saw "Braveheart," you saw what my descendants were like. Scotland has a heritage of great preachers, but the light went out long ago. I hope God in His grace stokes the embers again.

My grandpa was born in Glasgow just after the turn of the century. His father was an alcoholic who worked and drank. My grandpa told me his mother would take him down to the bar and set him on a stool while she cleaned the bar where his father had been the night before. My grandpa left Scotland at about 14 years of age by himself to come to America. He passed through Ellis Island, stayed in New York City while he completed school, then settled in Detroit to work in the automotive industry. He became somewhat like his father until, at the age of forty, he accepted Jesus as his savior.

He was radically changed. He became a man of resolve, dedicated to spreading the gospel of Jesus Christ to all who would listen. He and Grandma became active in Bible churches, teaching, helping, and working with kids in an organization called "Child Evangelism Fellowship." At the age of sixty, my grandpa made a decision to retire early from the Ford Motor Corporation, go back to Scotland, and use "Child Evangelism Fellowship" to win Scottish kids to Christ.

He did this for about 13 years until my grandma got sick; she had Alzheimer's disease. He brought her back to the states where she died. He died at the age of 86 of a heart attack. He was a great grandfather, and he left his grandchildren a great spiritual heritage.

Here's the point, what the Lord told me: *"John, make it a priority to finish well."*

What about you? Do you sit around the coffee shop and talk about the weather, or do you want to live for Christ in a meaningful way right up to the end, like Adrian Rogers, who passed away in 2006, or Billy Graham, who is still serving the Lord in his late 80s? Frankly, I love to play golf and fish as much as the next guy, but I want to finish well like the Apostle Paul, who said in 2 Timothy 4:6–8:

> *For I am already being poured out like a drink offering, and the time has come for my departure. I have fought the good fight, I have finished the race, I have kept the faith. Now there is in store for me the crown of righteousness, which the Lord, the righteous Judge, will award to me on that day—and not only to me, but also to all who have longed for his appearing (NIV).*

I hope my grandchildren will be able to look back and say "Grandpa John left us a godly heritage. He was a great grandpa."

Let me encourage you to finish well.

. . . being confident of this very thing, that He who has begun a good work in you will complete it until the day of Jesus Christ . . .

PHILIPPIANS 1:6 (NKJV)

Being Honest with Myself:

Do I plan to run the race and finish well, or will my later years be "all about me?" Is it my goal to pass a godly heritage on to the coming generations?

Be a Servant

*W*here did fifty years go? I thought as I sat in my truck. *It wasn't that long ago my kids were born; it was only thirty years ago I got married.* I sat there reminiscing about living for half a century.

Now, I was still 49, but my wife had triggered these thoughts when she informed me that she was throwing me a fiftieth birthday party and was letting me know in advance so I could help her with the list and the setup and menu.

As I sat there in my pickup that day, the Lord said, *"John, there's something I want you to do at your birthday party."*

"Okay, Lord," I answered. "What do you want me to do?"

"At your party there will be cake and ice cream. When it comes time to serve it, instead of you being served, I want you to serve all your friends."

I thought about that. The Lord said, *"I don't want you to say a word about this, not even to Brenda, until a day or two before the party."*

I told Him I would do it, then went on to spend time with Jesus.

As time does, the three weeks went by quickly, and while we had planned to have a backyard picnic of sorts, the Lord informed me several days in advance that it was going to rain, so my friend John Cunningham ("Sparky") said we could have the party in a building he owned. That was a relief, since almost one hundred people had been invited, and most had accepted.

May 11 rolled around, and I turned fifty. It turned cold for May and started raining, so being inside was nice. Sparky's son Kip had started an upscale car business, selling mostly BMWs, Mercedes, and

Porches, so Kip had some nice cars displayed, and my wife went with the "Hot Wheels" theme. Both old and new friends showed up, and everyone had a great time.

When it came time to serve the cake and ice cream, the Lord said, *"John, it is time to tell your friends."*

I gathered this wonderful group of people together and told them what God had told me to do.

Two or three friends, along with my wife, put the dessert on plates, and I served all eighty plus friends who came to celebrate my fiftieth birthday with me.

In today's world, serving is a word to which only lip-service is paid. But the King of Kings has called us, those who believe, to have the hearts of servants. Quite honestly, I look forward to serving Jesus one day in Heaven. I figure I had better get to practicing now.

> *Jesus called them together and said, "You know that the rulers of the Gentiles lord it over them, and their high officials exercise authority over them. Not so with you. Instead, whoever wants to become great among you must be your servant, and whoever wants to be first must be your slave—just as the Son of Man did not come to be served, but to serve, and to give his life as a ransom for many."*

> MATTHEW 20:25–28 (NIV)

Being Honest with Myself:

Have I become a servant to others, or do I prefer others to serve me?

A Lesson from the World's Oldest Profession

n 1991, I traveled to New York City to visit my brother Bill, who was dying of AIDS, as I mentioned in a previous story. The visit was bittersweet for me. I spent long hours in the AIDS ward listening to the screams and cries of patients who were devastated by this horrible disease.

During the week I was there, I found myself needing some spiritual refreshment. Having heard about Times Square Church, I decided to visit Wednesday or Thursday night. The church is on 42nd Street in Times Square, which at that time was a center for prostitution and every sexual fantasy one could imagine. Today Times Square is delightful to visit, thanks to former Mayor Giuliani, who spearheaded an effort to clean up the area.

The church service was about two hours long, and when it was finished, I decided to walk back to my brother's apartment where I was staying. New York is truly a city that doesn't sleep, with thousands of people walking somewhere even late at night. I had not walked but a few blocks when I found myself behind two young prostitutes escorted by a tall, good-looking businessman who looked to be in his mid-thirties. He was dressed to the nines, very professional-looking; the prostitutes were dressed in hot pants, fishnet stockings, low-cut blouses and high heels. Normally I would have walked around the trio and continued on my way, but I sensed the Lord wanted me to follow the three.

Walking several blocks, the man stopped at a corner ATM machine to get cash. He had to wait for a couple of people in line and step over a vagabond trying to find shelter. Instead of walking on past him, I stopped about ten feet away from the girls and took a look as they milled around waiting for their escort to come out with his cash. The girls were giggling about something, and I could not help but notice that they were very young. The older girl looked like she was about 18 or 19, but the younger girl looked to be about 13 or 14 years old; she was bouncy and innocent-looking. I watched them, and the Lord began to speak to me.

"John, what do you see?" He asked.

I remembered seeing that the man had a wedding ring on his finger. "I see a married man getting ready to commit adultery."

"What else do you see?"

I stated the obvious. "Well, I see two girls who are selling themselves for money." I looked at the younger girl and thought how truly child-like she looked. As I looked at her, the Lord spoke to me again.

"This is her first time."

I stared at the younger girl, stunned.

"John, I want to ask you this," the Lord said. *"Does sin bother you? Do you notice sin?"*

I stood there, still reeling.

"John, sin cost Me My Son; sin sent Him to the Cross." God asked me again: *"Does sin bother you?"*

As I stood there, my heart was unexpectedly broken for them and for what they were going to do, and I began to weep. I suddenly understood God's heart on the issue of sin.

The two girls began to notice that I was staring at them. I began to say, "Don't do this. Please, don't do this." But the older girl pulled the younger one away, the man came with his cash, and the three proceeded into the lobby of a nearby hotel.

I walked back to my brother's apartment, heartbroken. I never forgot that night in New York.

So I ask you now what the Lord asked me: What do you see? When you see sin, do you give it much thought? *Does sin bother you?*

My fear is that the church in America is becoming desensitized to evil. My prayer for us is that we would remember Romans 6:23: "For the wages of sin is death, but the gift of God is eternal life in Christ Jesus our Lord" (NIV).

> *To fear the Lord is to hate evil . . .*
>
> PROVERBS 8:13 (NIV)

> *. . . for all have sinned and fall short of the glory of God, and are justified freely by his grace through the redemption that came by Christ Jesus.*
>
> ROMANS 3:23–24 (NIV)

Being Honest with Myself:

Do I excuse sinful behavior in myself and others? Do I say "Oh, well," and look away?

Under the Bridge

Most of the time, you do not know where they have come from; if they tell you where, it is probably not completely true. They are just passing through. They are men and women who, because of alcohol, drugs, bad marriages, and every other reason under the sun, decide to give up and hit the roads and rails of America. They pass from one city to another, stopping to get food and rest at various missions in our cities. They are the homeless.

Jeff was another in a long line of people who have passed through my life. He asked me for a day's work; he said he would do anything, but he just needed money before catching the rail to Memphis. Jeff was not comfortable at the missions; he preferred cardboard boxes with a couple of old blankets he had received form the Salvation Army.

"So where's home this week, Jeff?" I asked him. Jeff said he was staying under a bridge off Grant Street. His story was one I am sure my friend Jim at Victory Mission had heard a thousand times. Jeff had been born down south in Bayou country. His dad was an alcoholic for as long as he could remember. He beat Jeff and his mother most nights. Jeff had quit school and run away from home to find work off the coast. He worked on oil derricks in the gulf; the money was good, but he did not like the solitude. He began working different jobs on the mainland, meeting different women until he thought he'd met the right one. It was not long before he caught her with someone else. After a bad fight, Jeff took off. He was still running.

Our friends Rich and Becky were in from Long Island, New York.

They had been our neighbors when we were in our early twenties. My wife fixed a wonderful meal, and I asked her for a plate to take to Jeff under the bridge. I knew the Lord's direction was clear: take Jeff some food and share the gospel with him. I asked Rich to go with me.

"Where are we going?" he asked.

I told him we were just going to take some food to a guy I met. Rich was not that big of a guy, but he was athletic—he had a black belt in Tae Kwan Do. I knew he would be a good companion for where we were going.

I drove over to a liquor store and parked. It was Sunday afternoon, so the store was closed. With the food in one hand and a Bible in my back pocket, I made my way with Rich down through the weeds under the bridge on Grant Street. Sure enough, true to his word, Jeff was sitting on some cardboard, just staring into space. I greeted him, "Hi, Jeff."

"Hi, John."

"I brought you some food; my wife made it. And I got you a Gideon Bible. My father-in-law is a member." I stood for a moment and then asked, "Do you mind if I sit down?"

"Nah," he said, "Go ahead. Sorry I don't have better conditions."

I told him it was okay and sat down. Rich stood and kept watch.

I did not belabor the point but said, "Jeff, you know Jesus loves you. I just came to remind you and give you that Bible. Can you read?"

He said, "Okay, I guess."

So I gave him the Bible and showed him where I wrote his name on it. Like so many people, it seemed to go in one ear and out the other. I reiterated the gospel story to him. He sat there, picking at his food. I put my hand on his shoulder and told him I would see him later, knowing full well I never would.

Several other vagabonds were starting to come out of the different hideaways, probably wanting some of the bounty. Rich was getting nervous, and I was getting nowhere. But seeds were sown; the Lord had told me to take Jeff some food and tell him about the gospel, and I had. Rich and I walked out from under the bridge, through the abandoned trash, up through the weeds and to the liquor store where we had parked. We got in the car and drove home.

> The Spirit of the Sovereign Lord is on me, because the Lord has anointed me to preach good news to the poor. He has sent me to bind up the brokenhearted, to proclaim freedom for the captives and release from darkness for the prisoners . . .
>
> ISAIAH 61:1 (NIV)

Being Honest with Myself:

Do I listen when God speaks to me about someone in dire straits? Am I obedient to Him when He calls me?

A Church Destroyed

S ome stories are just hard to tell, and this is one of those stories.

It all started when a small group of us traveled to the James Robinson Bible conference in Dallas, Texas. Two of the people we traveled with were the pastor and his wife. I really do not remember all the speakers, except Arthur Blessit and James Robinson, but God was there in a powerful way. Thousands of people came needing renewal in their lives. Our pastor was admittedly one of those people; he was tired and burnt out.

The church was really an average church until God changed that pastor. When he and his wife came back to Springfield, the presence of God came with them to our little Baptist church of 93 people. Pastor's first sermon was entitled "Jesus or Religion." People started coming in droves, and before long it was literally standing room only. Pure worship and praise were part of every service. People were being saved and healed; broken hearts and marriages were being mended. I was excited to be a part of such growth. The church was growing to the point we needed new facilities. Finally, the new church was built. It sat three times the amount of people in the old building. Within the first few months, the auditorium was full. God was moving in mighty ways.

I will not go into great detail about different things that took place as Satan launched an attack against the church. From my perspective, one of the things that led to the church's demise was a lack of humble prayer; those prayers in humility were replaced with "prayer" telling God what to do. Worship from a pure heart was replaced with

"Kingdom Now"—but God is looking for pure worshippers who worship in spirit and in truth (John 4:23). We seemed, in my opinion, to have left our first love and focused our attention on the gifts rather than the giver.

I will never forget one night when I was running late. As I walked down the long corridor to the auditorium, the Spirit of the Lord stopped me dead in my tracks just before walking into the sanctuary. I stood there and watched people standing on the chairs, dancing along the walls . . . the praise and worship was so loud the room was shaking. I started to walk in and sit down, when that wonderful voice spoke:

"John, I am going to destroy this church. Go home and intercede for it."

I turned and drove back home, where I knelt and prayed for over three hours.

"I have heard you, but I will not save the church," said the Lord.

He never told me why He did what He did, and I certainly would not have the foggiest idea. I know there are as many opinions as there were people in the church. The Lord owes me no explanation. I can only say what I observed.

This is not an easy story for me to write. Today the church, which once ran about 1,400 people, does not exist; the building is home to a private school. I know God is a jealous God, and He will not bless anything that does not glorify Him. This includes praise and prayer that are done in the flesh.

> *The word of the Lord came to me, "Son of man, if a country sins against me by being unfaithful and I stretch out my hand against it to cut off its food supply and send famine upon it and kill its men and their animals, even if these three men—Noah, Daniel and Job—were in it, they could save only themselves by their righteousness, declares the Sovereign Lord."*
>
> EZEKIEL 14:12–14 (NIV)

Being Honest with Myself:

When God looks on my heart, what kind of heart is He seeing?

January 3, 1980

D ates are important. People celebrate birthdays and anniversaries. Every cemetery is replete with tombstones marking who lies there, the date of their birth and death. Our calendars are covered with dates that are set aside to honor a president or special holiday . . . everything from Martin Luther King Day to World AIDS Day. In fact, not a week goes by that a date is not set aside to honor or remember someone or something. January 3, 1980 is a special spiritual date for me, and for me it is, as President Roosevelt declared, "A day that will live in infamy."

This story really starts years earlier, with my fundamentalist religious upbringing. I developed some very unhealthy spiritual attitudes. I was not brought into Sunday school and taught emphatically to be racist or self-righteous or legalistic because I happened to be part of God's "special denomination." But what I heard at the church socials, the talk among the men as they smoked outside the church before going inside to sing "Amazing Grace," programmed my mind. As a kid growing up in Kentucky, I can still remember the conversations men would have before church. They went something like this:

"Jim, how's your tobacco coming along this year?"

Jim would give the same answer, depending on the weather or the worms: "Pretty good, I'd say. Yeah, it's been looking good."

"How's the distillery fairing over in Bardstown, Leroy?" Bill would ask.

"Fine, just fine. Going to have a great batch of bourbon this year, I can tell you that," Leroy would answer.

Then there were the conversations about the racetracks, politics, and blacks. Everyone had an opinion, and everyone tried to wedge theirs in before the singing started. That is when they would flick their Camel cigarettes out into the grass and take their seats for Sunday service.

My parents, especially my mom, thought this was disgusting talk and commented on it most Sundays over pot roast or in the restaurant in which we were eating. So for about 12 years of religious life, I saw people who went to church on Sunday but lived different lives Monday through Saturday. On the other hand, I saw the righteous but legalistic way that said "my way or the highway, and the highway leads to hell." Freedom in Christ was never mentioned, because no one really knew what that meant. So I grew up believing the song "We Will Work 'til Jesus Comes," and I set out to do my best for God in hopes that I would have at least one crown to cast at His feet when Heaven called me home.

My mother was staunch in her beliefs about sin: don't do it. So I set out to be the best person I could be. My motto could have been, "Don't drink, don't smoke, don't chew, and don't go with the girls who do. Work for Jesus and above all else, come out from among them and be ye separated saith the Lord." The problem with all this was that I developed a self-righteous attitude and a spiritual headiness that I justified to myself. This went along year after year until God in His grace decided it was time to change Johnny's attitude. And how do you suppose He would do that? Well, in my case, it was letting me crash in my flesh.

At about twenty years of age, I started doing things I recognized as sinful—a little here and a little there—until I got to the place where I could justify any behavior. Finally, I decided I could not live this Christian life anymore, anyway, so why keep trying? At age 27, I quit going to church and started drinking, looking at dirty magazines, excusing R-rated movies that took the Lord's name in vain, and cursing because that is what everybody did, anyway. And heck, they were all having a good time . . . or so I thought.

I will not tell you that was a great time for me, because it was not. I was grieving the Holy Spirit that had possessed me back in Kentucky when He found me at Gethsemane Baptist church at the age of nine—that same church where men used their zippers to strike matches that lit their cigarettes. But God was faithful and showed up because the pastor preached the gospel, and God always honors His Word.

By the end of 1979, I was under extreme conviction about my life and the direction it was headed. I am not sure how my wife found them, but she came across a set of cassette tapes by Dr. Charles Stanley on brokenness. For five days while she was preparing to go to work, she would play them in the bathroom. My response was always the same: "Brenda! Turn the tapes off; I'm trying to sleep." All I had done was gripe on all five days she had listened to the tapes. The sixth tape was played on January 3, 1980. When I woke up at about 3:00 p.m. (I worked the graveyard shift then), I can only say it had to be God, because I was by myself in the kitchen, and I put that sixth tape in and started listening to it. The only phrase I remember hearing was "If God has to, He will use the dearest thing in your life to get your attention."

When I heard that, I began to weep uncontrollably. The Spirit of God flooded the kitchen as I repented of my sins and told God it was my fault and I was sorry. I still remember looking at the clock on the stove; it was 4:30 p.m. when I finally, after all those years, came clean with God. He cleaned me inside and out and filled me with His Spirit. I could not explain it then, but I remember His voice: *"John, I will live this Christian life through you by my power; you cannot do it alone."* That was 22 years ago, and I can tell you that He is still my best friend and Lord of my life. I am a huge proponent of grace now, amazing grace from a God who finds worthless people like me and changes them from dead men into people whose lives are filled with God. I am not proud of any past behavior or present behavior that might not be in sync with God, but I am not ashamed to be numbered among those heroes of the faith who blew it—from Adam to Moses to Peter.

> *And such were some of you. But you were washed, but you were sanctified, but you were justified in the name of the Lord Jesus and by the Spirit of our God.*
>
> 1 CORINTHIANS 6:11 (NKJV)

Being Honest with Myself:

Am I like one of His sheep who has gone astray?

Tear It Up

A s I already mentioned, January 3, 1980 was a hallmark day in my life. This was only the first step in what has become a life walk with the Living Savior. My wife came home the evening of January 3 and could only stare at first; the change was more than she could believe. She had fasted and prayed for me for five days several months earlier. Although I had not noticed the dramatic transformation in her life, God had a plan. His plan was that Brenda and I were going to travel this journey together, not apart.

For three days after January 3, I could not stop crying. Joy for what God had done in my life would flood my soul. I had been radically changed by Him. I remember calling my friend Frank in Harrison, Arkansas, and sharing with him what had happened to me. The mentoring could wait; it was time to celebrate the homecoming of a lost sheep.

A common practice of shepherds in Jesus' time was to break the leg of a lamb that kept wandering off. The shepherd would then reset it and carry the lamb on his shoulders until the leg healed. The period of time in which the shepherd would carry the lamb would cause the lamb to bond to the shepherd; by the time the leg healed, the lamb only wanted to follow the master. It would not wander off again. That is how I felt. I was not the least bit interested in going anywhere except to the Lord. He had "broken my leg."

My problem before had been that I knew about God; I just did not know Him personally. After January 3, God and I were like a grandfather and grandson: the grandfather takes his little grandson to the park to play on the merry-go-round, buys him an ice cream cone, then sits on a bench to listen to the little guy jabber about nothing. The grandpa enjoys every minute of it because it is his grandson. That is the way it was for several days between us.

About the fourth or fifth day, the Lord spoke to me very clearly: *"John, get out some paper and a pen and sit down at the table."*

I went and got a legal pad and a pen and sat down at the kitchen table.

"John, I want you to write down every sin that my Spirit leads you to write," he said.

"Okay, Lord," I replied, and I began to write down sins I had committed, beginning when I was only a child and lied to my mother, stole baseball cards from the store, went to see the "Gypsy Rose Lee" movie and was sorry I got caught, not sorry that I did it! Sin after sin I recorded until I had two legal pad pages filled. I sat there feeling so bad about them, not knowing what to say. The Lord seemed to let me stew over the list for a couple of minutes. Then He spoke:

"John, tear them up. I don't remember them anymore, and neither should you."

I jumped out of the chair and tore those yellow pages into as many tiny pieces as I could, then walked over to the trashcan and threw them away. God had given me a new beginning.

> As far as the east is from the west, so far has he removed our transgressions from us. As a father has compassion on his children, so the Lord has compassion on those who fear Him; for He knows how we are formed, He remembers that we are dust.
>
> PSALM 103:12–14 (NIV)

Being Honest with Myself:

Have I committed sins against a holy God that I have not confessed? Are there things in my past or present for which I need to ask forgiveness? The Lord says to write them down, confess, and repent, then go toward the high calling.

A Friend

cannot say I remember the first time I met him; it might have been over a church dinner, since both of us have wives who are quintessential hostesses. It might have been because our sons were drawn like magnets to each other at the age of three and are still friends today at the age of 25. But I do remember the first time I saw him. We were both in our mid-twenties. My wife and I had begun attending the same church as he and his wife. He was sitting behind us, and when I turned to look around, he caught my attention. At that moment, the Lord whispered to me: *"John, this man will become your best friend."* I cannot say I thought about that too much, but time has proven God to be true.

Our wives laugh because we are the odd couple. When we met, I worked in a factory and he owned a factory. He earned a Master's degree, and I never finished college. Most people view him as Roger Rabbit and me as the slowest person they know. But God saw us as two men who would travel a spiritual highway together; two totally different men like Peter and Paul of the New Testament. One a fisherman, the other a rabbi and scholar, they were opposites with the same purpose: to know Christ, the author and finisher of our faith.

I have been blessed by my friend's business integrity, his keen mind and sharp wit, but mostly I have been blessed by his relentless pursuit of Christ. Both of us will turn 52 this year, and I still enjoy his dry sense of humor and the seemingly endless funny stories he has told through the years. Our families have been on vacations together to Florida; we have taken our wives to Canada on anniversaries. We have floated with our sons in Colorado and with other friends in

Africa. We have been on many mission trips together, always coming home with different hearts and sore bodies. We have wept through trials and endured long nights at hospitals awaiting news about one another's families. We have stood over grills and cooked countless hamburgers together. We have fasted and prayed for our sons and rejoiced in the beauty and grace God has given our daughters. If the Lord tarries, I suppose we will grow old together and watch our grandchildren play together in our backyards. The years will tell the story of two men brought together by God who ran a good race and finished the course Jesus had put before them.

The people of the world cry out for friends. Many people live lonely lives, much like the song that says "the tears of a clown, when there's no one around." Over the years, I have observed a myriad of people who live lonely lives with no real friends, people who live in quiet desperation. Let me encourage you to be the person that Jesus talked about, the one who lets his or her light shine before men, that they might see your good works and glorify the Father in Heaven (Matthew 5).

I will always be thankful to the Lord for putting in my life Sparky and all my other dear friends. I leave you with this: reach out to people and be their friend. People need you, and you will reap dividends, both present and eternal.

> *This is my commandment, that you love one another just as I have loved you. Greater love has no one than this, than to lay down one's life for his friends. You are My friends if you do whatever I command you.*
>
> JOHN 15:12–14 (NKJV)

Being Honest with Myself:

There are many people who need a good friend. Am I the one Jesus is looking for to use as a blessing in someone else's life?

Krispy Kremes

This story happened recently, but God seems to be telling me, *"John, I want you to share this; there is a great truth in it."*

My daughter's birthday is February 17. Her mother and I told her that we would take her up the road to Kansas City to spend the night and eat at the Cheesecake Factory, a great restaurant located on the Plaza.

Now the whole time we were driving up there (and it was a two and a half hour drive), I was thinking, *I don't want cheesecake; I want a Krispy Kreme donut!*

I was raised in South Carolina for part of my life, and there was a Krispy Kreme donut shop about a half mile from my house. If you have never had Krispy Kreme donuts—run, don't walk to the nearest Krispy Kreme and get a hot donut coming off the conveyor belt. They melt in your mouth!

After eating at the Cheesecake Factory that day, I resisted all the server's suggestions for cheesecake, my mind on those donuts. I told the family we would get Krispy Kremes the next morning for breakfast, and we went back to the hotel for a night's rest. About 4:30 a.m. I woke up and thought I would go and pray. I am so used to praying in my vehicle that I headed downstairs to ask the valet to get my Blazer. As I was waiting, I thought about those donuts. The more I thought about them, the more I wanted them. I looked up the address to Krispy Kreme and asked the front desk for directions. Since I was tired, I misunderstood the directions and ended up going the wrong way. After about thirty minutes of driving, I stopped to get gas and ask directions again.

"You're headed the wrong way," the attendant said, pointing me in the right direction. I got in my Blazer and headed back toward Krispy Kreme donuts. Somewhere along the way I got turned around again and had to stop at a grocery store to get further directions.

"Yeah, Krispy Kreme . . . that's about three miles west then turn south on Metcalf for about one mile. It will be on your right before you get to I-35."

Finally, I made it to the greatest donut store America ever produced (well, in this southern boy's opinion). They were making fresh ones, so I bought my coffee and half a dozen donuts. Now, my intention was to eat three and take three back to the hotel for my wife and daughter. I had killed almost an hour getting to Krispy Kreme and spent another twenty minutes getting back downtown. By the time I pulled into Union Station to read and pray under the lights, it was close to 6:15 a.m.

I opened that box of Krispy Kremes and, with my hot cup of coffee, I sat there and tried to read the Bible. I thought, *This is going to be the best morning of prayer ever!* And then I proceeded to eat every one of those donuts. By the time I finished reading the Bible, the sugar hit me and I got tired. I thought I'd go back to the room and sleep some more; after all, it was Saturday. I got rid of all the evidence: the coffee cup, the crumbs, the box. I was too embarrassed to tell my family I had eaten their donuts.

By the time I returned to the room, the sugar had really done a job on me; I was exhausted. I had not eaten any sugar for over a week; I was doing the Atkins diet at the time. I thought I would sneak into the room, but everyone was awake, and their first question was: "Can we get Krispy Kremes for breakfast?"

"I'm too tired to talk about it; let me sleep some more," I said, "Wake me up at 9:00."

"Okay," my wife said. "Then we can get Krispy Kremes."

"Right. Wake me up at 9:00 or 9:30."

Nine o'clock rolled around too early. I got out of bed and headed slowly to the bathroom. My wife said it was time to get donuts. I was still full from the six I had already eaten, and the sugar had not worn off.

"I will tell you what," I said, "let's wait until this afternoon when we take Jenny to the mall in Overland Park."

My wife and daughter just looked at each other like "Is Dad okay?" My wife made the comment that she was proud of me for sticking to my diet plan.

That afternoon, we finally pulled into the donut store. I ate three more donuts.

"These sure are good," I said. "Couldn't wait to get here."

We bought some for friends and family and headed back south to Springfield. That evening, with a guilt-ridden conscience, I confessed to my wife that I had not quite told the truth about the Krispy Kremes. She was both amused and outraged, but she forgave me.

The next morning I headed out to pray without any of the world's finest donuts, only a cup of coffee. As I pulled into the church parking lot, the Lord spoke.

"John, we need to talk about the Krispy Kreme donuts."

I was not sure where that was going, so I said, "Lord, what about the donuts?"

"John," the Lord said, *"you know that Krispy Kreme is coming to Springfield this year, and you can't be going by there every morning before you pray."*

I thought about that for a moment.

"First, you will gain weight," he continued. *"Second, you must learn to buffet the flesh, or you will be on a sugar high every day. Do you understand?"*

"Yes, sir, I understand."

He finished with, *"John, I don't care if you eat a Krispy Kreme, but pick one day a week and make it a treat. Krispy Kremes are not one of the food groups."*

Now I learned a lesson that week. No matter how long you walk with God, the flesh will still war against the spirit. What about you; what drives you? Is it lust? Porn? Greed? Drugs? Power? Food? Donuts? It doesn't matter; there is only one answer: Jesus Christ. He alone sets us free. We have to listen to Him, and it is a moment-by-moment thing.

What a wretched man I am! Who will rescue me from this body of death? Thanks be to God—through Jesus Christ our Lord!

ROMANS 7:24–25 (NIV)

Being Honest with Myself:

Am I more controlled by the Spirit or by my flesh?

Beauty

Over the years, I have found it both interesting and exciting how God accomplishes His will. This particular story is one that, quite frankly, I had to think about writing for two weeks before I acted, because what God had asked me to do seemed very unusual to me. My family and I had gone to church on this particular Sunday. Nothing was unusual about the sermon that week, but what happened at church that day intrigues me even now.

As I sat in church, I happened to notice a young lady, about twenty years old, sitting across the aisle four or five rows in front of my wife and me. The angle at which she was sitting gave me a good view of her profile; for some reason, I could not stop looking at this young lady. Now staring at someone is usually inappropriate, but staring at a young lady in church with your wife sitting beside you, well, that is hard to explain! Finally, the Lord spoke to me:

"John, I have given this young lady the grace of beauty. I want you to tell her that."

When church was over, I left and went home with my wife, not saying a word to that young woman or my own red-headed beauty.

The very next Sunday, I found my way to the same section we usually sit in. Before the music had started, I sat down and began to look around. I noticed the same young lady sitting in about the same spot as she had before. She was sitting alone, and I noticed that she did not seem to know anyone sitting beside her. As had happened the previous Sunday, the Lord simply spoke the same words to me:

"John, I have given this young lady the grace of beauty. I want you to tell her that."

Okay, Lord, I thought. *After the service, I will tell her.*

The service ended, and I made my way over to her. I asked her if I could sit down beside her; I explained that the Lord had told me to tell her something. She of course looked at me like a calf looks at a new gate, and I could hardly blame her. Here I was, a complete stranger who was years older than her, and I was telling her I had a word from the Lord for her. She probably thought, *You don't know me well enough to tell me 'thus saith the Lord.'* I introduced myself; she did the same.

"The Lord told me to tell you this," I said, "He wants you to know that He has given you the grace of beauty." I told her that I did not have any idea why He asked me to tell her, but I was convinced He wanted me to, and I was happy to relay the message, which I reiterated. She did not really respond except to say thanks. I left for Sunday dinner.

I did not see her again until the next September. I was walking down the hall at church, and behind me I heard a voice: "Mom, that's him; Mom, that's the man."

I turned around, and there she was with the biggest smile, walking toward me with another woman, her mother, I guessed. She was beaming.

"Hi," I said to her mother, "I'm John Gordon."

She introduced herself as well and said, "I appreciate what you did for my daughter."

The young woman spoke up: "John, I won!"

"Won what?" I asked.

"I won two beauty contests this summer!" She explained that she had thought about entering but hesitated, thinking they were all about vanity and would not be appropriate for a Christian. God had confirmed through me that He wanted her to participate. She had entered two contests in Missouri. One of them was the State Fair pageant.

"I was just the messenger boy; that's all," I said as they expressed thanks again. I did not see her again after that; maybe she moved on to another church. But I will never forget the twenty year old girl to whom God gave the gift of beauty.

Esther 2:7 says that Esther was both lovely and beautiful. The Bible records others, like Rachel and David, who were beautiful people, and God used that beauty for His glory. However, we live in a world that has made an idol out of beauty and made gods out of the attractive. No matter how God made you, I know this: God does not make junk. You are fearfully and wonderfully made.

> *I will praise You, for I am fearfully and wonderfully made;*
> *marvelous are Your works, and that my soul knows very well.*

PSALM 139:14 (NKJV)

Being Honest with Myself:

Am I content with the way God has made me? Do I spend an inordinate amount of time on the body, neglecting the inner man?

Pray for a Hero

f hero worship was ever in vogue, I suppose that would be the day and age in which we live. A person cannot go very far without noticing a shirt or jacket with a product or a sports hero being touted by avid fans. People display emblems on their vehicles or bodies that say, in effect, "my hero."

First you have your sports heroes: people at the top of their game. Then there are the entertainment heroes: rock stars with their groupies and screaming fans. Then the actors and actresses: stars who are idolized by their adoring fans who would move heaven and earth for one glimpse of their idol. Of course, there are business heroes: men and women who have achieved enormous success in the world and live rich lifestyles. One type of hero worship that has particularly bothered me is the fantasy hero: the kind created by artists using different mediums. These heroes find their way through slick marketing to millions of children's minds via comics, cartoons, computer games, web sites, movies, and even hamburger boxes. What a nice change it was during and after September 11 when people began to recognize ordinary citizens like police officers, firefighters, and military personnel as real American heroes.

The Bible is not without its heroes, but they are heroes of faith: people who did extraordinary deeds and lived extraordinary lives for God. They are mentioned throughout Scripture, from Genesis to Revelation. God lists many of these heroes together in Hebrews 11. My two personal favorites, besides Jesus, are Moses and the apostle Peter. I like Moses because it is said that he knew God face to face, and God talked to him as a man talks to his friend (Exodus 33:11).

I like Peter because I can relate to him as a common man who did great things by the Holy Spirit who empowered him. He was a fisherman who gets laughed at a lot, but think about it: the man walked on water, raised the dead, saw Jesus in His glory at the transfiguration, wrote two books of the Bible, and paid his tax bill by taking money from a fish! And, most importantly, thousands of people came to know Christ through his sermons. That was around 2,000 years ago, but history still records people who have done great things in Jesus' name.

For example, I remember when the new century rolled over and A&E named the 100 most influential people in the last 1,000 years. Three of the top five were: Guttenberg, the inventor of the printing press, whose motivation was to print the Scriptures, Sir Isaac Newton, a God-honoring man who discovered gravity, and Martin Luther, the father of the Reformation. All throughout history, God has had His servants, men and women, who have lived the lives of heroes. How refreshing it is to the body of Christ to be able to look up to men and women even today who exemplify the Lord Jesus: people like Mother Teresa, Billy Graham, Adrian Rogers . . . the list is endless.

One particular hero of mine is Joe White, the owner of Kanakuk Kamps in Branson, Missouri. He is a wonderful fellow around my age who has the passionate pursuit of Jesus as his agenda, and he is a man who has always been kind to my son. The Lord clearly spoke to me one Wednesday afternoon, telling me that I had to go by my church's Wednesday night prayer meeting. Little did I know that Jesus wanted me to intercede for one of my heroes.

I walked in that night to our prayer meeting and sat down, listening to the pastor bring a brief message. Then he announced that a video presentation would be shown about this guy, Joe White. The video was of him building a cross on stage at a Promise Keepers convention, an illustrated sermon, very powerful. As the video was completed, they announced that Joe had been diagnosed with cancer, and he had come to ask for prayer from the church.

As I sat there next to my wife, a great burden from the Lord arose in me, and God said,

"John, I want you to pray for Joe; that is why I brought you here tonight."

Great faith arose in me, and I knew God would hear my prayer. I waited for several people to finish talking with Joe and praying with him, and then I made my way down to see my friend and hero, Joe White. The details of what was said might not be important, but God did ask me to do one thing:

"John, put your face on the floor and intercede for this man."

Facedown on the carpet, I begged God for Joe's health. He heard my prayer, and said, *"John, my strength is made perfect in weakness."* When He said that, I went home.

As for Joe, I do not get to see him often, but I will always appreciate how he has been a true hero of the faith to me. And I will always appreciate the kindness he showed my son. Thanks, Joe.

God will at times give each of us burdens for individuals, groups, events, or something else. Let me encourage you to take that burden before the Lord and intercede for whatever God puts on your heart. God wants us to bear one another's burdens, not pass them around to everyone else to avoid responsibility. You are probably the one whom God has chosen to make the biggest difference in someone's life through intercession.

> *We always thank God for all of you, mentioning you in our prayers. We continually remember before our God and Father your work produced by faith, your labor prompted by love, and your endurance inspired by hope in our Lord Jesus Christ.*
>
> 1 THESSALONIANS 1:2–3 (NIV)

Being Honest with Myself:

Is my hero first and foremost Jesus? Do I have good and godly heroes . . . or is my hero ME?

Nobody

The trip to Honduras was an exhausting one. The weather there was hot, over one hundred degrees, and the wind blew incessantly at about twenty miles per hour. We had no ice, so the water we drank was about eighty degrees in the shade. The best Coke I have ever had was when one of the missionaries drove fifty miles to a larger town and brought back ice-cold Cokes. Several of the men were dropping from heat exhaustion; we happened to have a medic on the trip who kept very busy. Pigs, chickens, and mangy dogs roamed free, hanging around the camp waiting for a morsel of food. During all of this, my buddy and I were cooking three meals a day and cleaning. However, keeping things even remotely clean was impossible. I remember going to bed with at least a quarter inch of dirt in the tent. In spite of all this, I never heard anyone complain.

During the five-day stint, I helped the men, took care of the camp, cooked the meals, cleaned up the meals, and tried to love on twenty or more kids twelve hours a day. I took food to the women, cut blocks, hauled water, shoveled mud, cleaned the outhouse, cleaned out the tent, and kept the Gatorade flowing to exhausted workers. At night we gave out candy. On the last day we built a swing set for the kids, the first one they had ever had in the village.

Now our church had sent a fellow to film all our work so the church members could see what had been accomplished. I have to admit that, two weeks later when I went to church to see the video presentation, the thought on my mind was, *I wonder what they will show me doing.* My mind was racing through the five days and all the duties I had performed.

The lights went out, the church hushed, and they showed the tape. I waited until the end—but I wasn't on there! I was shocked. The only one not on the video was me! I said, "Lord, that's not fair!" I hashed over all the chores I had done. He did not say a word. I sat there trying to look spiritual as the choir sang a special song.

At that time, I had volunteered to pray on Sunday evenings, so I had to get up and walk down the stairs to the pastor's office. I had no sooner reached the stairwell when the Lord's presence stopped me in my tracks.

"John, I want to ask you a question," the Lord said.

"What's that, Lord?"

"Will you be a nobody for me?"

I must have stood there for at least two minutes before I replied.

"Yes, Lord, I'll be a nobody for you."

I went to that prayer meeting, no longer worried about the video or any future videos ever again.

As humans, we live many times for the privilege of "Show and Tell"; let me show you what *I* have done; let me tell you what *I* have accomplished. But to really gain Christ, we must first empty ourselves so that He might be our all in all.

> *Compared to the high privilege of knowing Christ Jesus as my Master, firsthand, everything I once thought I had going for me is insignificant—dog dung. I've dumped it all in the trash so that I could embrace Christ and be embraced by him.*
>
> PHILIPPIANS 3:7–8 (THE MESSAGE)

Being Honest with Myself:

Am I willing to take up my cross daily? Am I willing to be last and "die" to me that He might be seen in this world?

No More Babies!

ighteen months before the story I am about to tell you occurred, I had been through a crisis of belief. By God's grace I came down on God's side of the fence. So I set out to know more about God, about the "Jesus I never knew," as Philip Yancey put it. I got seminar-itis. In 1981, my wife Brenda and I made plans to attend a seminar in Atlanta, Georgia, at a church pastored by Charles Stanley.

If I remember correctly, the meetings lasted for three days, so we spent those nights at my parents' house in Roswell. The meetings were divided into two segments, morning and evening. One afternoon I had gone back to my mother's house between sessions to eat and clean up. After supper, I made my way upstairs to take a shower and get ready to return to downtown Atlanta for the evening session.

As I walked into the bedroom, the Lord came to me and said, *"John, I want you and Brenda to have another baby."*

For four years we had tried to have a child, and when our son was finally born, we discovered he was hearing-impaired. I loved my son deeply, but I had become angry with God. At that point in my life, I was still angry at Him! So without even thinking, I said, "No way! Thanks, but no thanks!"

The Lord came right back and said, *"John, listen to me. I want you and Brenda to have another baby."*

Our verbal exchange went on for about an hour, back and forth, as I thought of every reason not to bring another child into the world. This is the only time in my life God has ever wrestled with me over an issue for that amount of time.

Finally, the Lord said to me: "*Okay, John. If you are not going to obey me, then don't tell me you love me anymore.*"

That broke my resolve. I fell to my knees. "Okay, Lord," I consented. "If you want us to have another baby, we will have another baby. You know I love you."

It had taken four years for my wife to become pregnant with our son. Little did I know, she was already pregnant with our second child, who would be born the following February in 1982. I learned later that the Lord had already dealt with Brenda on this subject; He had asked her to have another baby several months earlier.

Before I left the room that day, the Lord spoke again: "*John, because you have obeyed me, this child will be special. I want this child, and this child will be special to me.*"

My daughter will turn 22 in a couple of weeks; she is a wonderful young woman. And God, being true to His word, has given her grace, wisdom, and beauty.

In Acts 26:28, King Agrippa says to the apostle Paul: "Almost thou persuadest me to be a Christian" (KJV). Don't let yourself say, "Almost, Lord . . . you persuade me *almost.*" If He asks something of you, He has your best interest at heart. You can trust Him.

> "*Has the Lord as great delight in burnt offerings and sacrifices, as in obeying the voice of the Lord? Behold, to obey is better than sacrifice, and to heed than the fat of rams.*"
>
> 1 SAMUEL 15:22 (NKJV)

Being Honest with Myself:

Am I willing to obey God even when it's tough or when it's opposed to what I want?

Little Things

I f we are Christians, the Bible admonishes us: "Do not be drunk with wine in which is dissipation; but be filled with the Spirit" (Ephesians 5:18, NKJV). There is no greater aspiration for believers than to "walk in the Spirit" and love God with all our heart, soul, and mind. This has been a consuming passion of mine since January 3, 1980.

While this has been my goal, I have many times fallen short and walked "in the flesh." The scriptures identify the world, the flesh, and the devil as being enemies of our "Spirit-walk." I have found through the years that this change of behavior comes about very subtly. I am walking in the Spirit and, almost without notice, I find myself walking in the flesh.

I do not mean getting involved in extremely sinful behavior, although that can happen to Christians given enough time away from God. I am talking about "little" things, like neglecting Bible-reading, having shorter and shorter times of prayer, getting too busy with all the cares of life until, before you know it, days turn into weeks and then months and, in some peoples' lives, years. This is where I found myself in December, 2003: burned out, tired, and unable to connect with the God I so dearly loved. The little foxes had stolen the grapes (Song of Solomon 2:15). I remember finally telling God that I was not running on all cylinders.

His comment to me was: *"I've noticed that."*

"Well, Lord," I said. "I'd like to come back." And I remember distinctly what He said:

"Draw near to me and I will draw near to you."

I recognized that verse—James 4:8. He did not finish the rest of the verse, but that hit me like a ton of bricks. I had to make a move to draw near to God; He was not going to zap me with lightning. He was not going to wave His hand and "poof!" make it better.

At the time, my father-in-law was in the hospital. He was very sick, and the outcome looked inevitable. He would soon go be with Jesus. This was a trying time for my wife, of course. We live about two good golf shots from a hospital, and my wife spent sometimes ten to twelve hours a day sitting with her father there. He died December 19, 2003. After this happened, I remember thinking: *I will start a fast on January 3, 2003, and fast until I get a breakthrough, no matter how long it takes.*

I ended up fasting for ten days. On the tenth day, Sunday, the church I attend had communion. The little cracker that represents the body of our Lord was the first food I had had in ten days. Right after the communion, the Lord said to me: *"I've heard your prayer; you can end the fast."* I felt closer to Him after that.

As I write this story, my wife is gone; she went to Oregon with her mother to attend the funeral of her aunt, and she has been gone a week today. Quite frankly, I miss her a lot. I do not like being without her. I miss sleeping with her, I miss her cooking, I miss talking to her. We have been together since we were eighteen.

The point: God does not like being out of fellowship with us, either. It bugs Him—aren't you glad it does? Second place irritates Him.

God does not like going all day or week without hearing from us much, if at all. He does not like seeing us so busy, hearing us say things like "I'll get around to praying tomorrow." He honestly misses that fellowship.

So what about you? Have the cares of this life, the "little things," robbed you of that wonderful relationship with God and His son, Jesus? Are you fleshly, worldly, or just busy? Do you sense a sputtering in your life, like bad gas in a car? Let me encourage you to stop and seek the Lord. He will let you find Him.

Seek the Lord while He may be found, call upon Him while He is near.

Isaiah 55:6 (NKJV)

Being Honest with Myself:

Have I let little things come in between me and Jesus?

The Defense Attorney

have always found it interesting how the Lord brings people together. It seems like people going along in life with no reason to ever meet one another suddenly find themselves looking each other in the eye, saying hello. Most of the time they are just passing by. Sometimes permanent bonds are formed. Such was the way it went in March of 2000 when my friend, Don, a circuit judge in my city, asked me to attend a new Bible study getting underway at Panera Bread.

The Bible study was to be mainly for professional people and was led by a very capable teacher, David, a federal defense attorney. David is an articulate man with keen insight into the scriptures and a gift for teaching. In spite of that, I balked at the notion, since I thought I would be the "odd man out." But I sensed the Lord nudging me to go.

I was in a hurry that first morning, and when I got out of my truck, I forgot my Bible. I thought I would just sit quietly and listen. The only seat available was next to a defense attorney by the name of Shawn Askinosie. The first thing I noticed about him was his Bible, which looked new. It still had the pages stuck together. I thought, *This guy never reads his Bible!* What I did not know, and what Shawn told me later, was that when he first saw me, he noticed that I did not even have a Bible. His first thought was, *Lord, I will probably have to share my Bible with this guy—if fact, he probably needs me to buy him a Bible.*

Now, Shawn is known around the country for his work in two very high-profile murder cases that he successfully defended. He has been featured on NBC's *Dateline*, has been named Defense Attorney of the Year in Missouri, and was named the Best Attorney in Springfield as featured in *417 Magazine*. My point is: the odds were about as good as walking on water that we would be friends. But God sees differently, and like so many times before, the great Savior of my soul wanted to teach me something—using a defense attorney.

Most people do not have high opinions of defense attorneys, and I did not know a lot of people who thought highly of Shawn. He defended accused murderers, thieves, drug dealers . . . well, you get the point. When one person I know, a church-goer, found out I was in the same Bible study, he told me candidly that he could not believe I could sit in the same room as Shawn.

As the weeks turned into months, though, I found myself drawn to Shawn. He truly was a man seeking God, a man who was open to the truth of Scripture and to the Lord's working in his life. The Lord had put a deep love in my heart for Shawn. Eventually, he became one of my dearest friends.

Months have now turned into years, but oh, how many times the Lord has reminded me that Jesus is my defense attorney. 1 Timothy 2:5–6 says:

> *For there is one God and one Mediator between God and men, the Man Christ Jesus, who gave Himself a ransom for all, to be testified in due time . . .* (NKJV).

When Satan, the accuser of the brethren, accuses me before God's holy throne, my great Heavenly Attorney intercedes and says "Father—that sin is paid in full." Jesus defends murderers and thieves and drug-dealers—"And such were some of you" (1 Corinthians 6:11, NKJV).

I am so glad I did not prejudge Shawn and run the other way. I would have missed knowing a wonderful, godly man. And besides, I highly doubt the rest of the disciples liked Matthew, the tax collector, when Jesus first called and introduced him.

> *Do not be deceived: Neither the sexually immoral nor idolaters nor adulterers nor male prostitutes nor homosexual offenders nor thieves nor the greedy nor drunkards nor slanderers nor swindlers*

will inherit the kingdom of God. And that is what some of you were. But you were washed, you were sanctified, you were justified in the name of the Lord Jesus Christ and by the Spirit of our God.

1 Corinthians 6:9–11 (NIV, emphasis mine)

Being Honest with Myself:

Do I tend to prejudge people before I get to know them?

The Gladiator

once heard a Jewish Rabbi say that a Biblical generation was 51.3 years. Anyone who was younger than this was still considered a young man. Anyone older than that was, well, let's just say . . . "seasoned." In 2004 I celebrated my 52nd birthday. I'll let you do the math.

Joel 2:28 says:

> And afterward, I will pour out my Spirit on all people. Your sons and daughters will prophesy, your old men will dream dreams, your young men will see visions (NIV).

The apostle Peter also quotes this verse in Acts 2:17.

Now, I'm a person who never remembers dreaming, and in the last 52 years, I couldn't tell you one dream I've ever had. That is, until the Lord gave this old man a dream just prior to my 52 birthday.

Here is that dream.

I was in a Roman Coliseum. I was dressed like a gladiator, holding a small round shield in my left hand and a sword clutched in my right. My helmet was metal. This wasn't my first time in the Coliseum to do battle. I had been there many times. Quite honestly, I was tired from the years of battle.

I entered the arena in anticipation. Thousands of onlookers began to cheer, but at the same time, thousands of others booed and hissed. I waited for my opponent to enter from the opposite side. As I waited, I looked above the Coliseum and saw countless spiritual beings anticipating the fight to come. Some of the beings were Heavenly. Others were the epitome of evil. Above them were the heavenly host, saints, angels, and the Lord Himself clothed in white.

Suddenly the doors crashed open across the arena. I looked over, and in stepped a great evil. I couldn't make out his face, but he was clothed with the world system, and Satan empowered him. He hated me because of my love for Jesus. He charged, his loathing almost tangible. The contest was on.

The fighting was intense. He struck me with blow after blow. I fought back as I had in the past, but I was tired and he was strong. Finally, he dealt a blow to my side that proved too much. I fell.

The evil thing gloated over my fallen body. The enemies of Heaven rejoiced over a saint who looked defeated. As the evil being turned to finish me off, I looked up and saw Jesus. Great power immediately entered my arm, and I turned to thrust my sword into the evil one's heart, finishing him for good.

The battle was over, but it would be my last. As I lay there on the arena floor with my eyes focused on Heaven, I realized I couldn't see the Lord.

Then with a rush, the gates opened again in the Coliseum, and in rode the Lord Himself, clothed in the brightest white, riding a pure white stallion. A hush came over the crowd. All of Heaven and earth was silent as He rode over to me. The Lord dismounted and bent down to pick me up. He smiled as He held me. His look was such that I finally understood His great love perfectly. I was overwhelmed with the love this great God had for me. I felt perfect peace and understanding as He held me.

Then He lay my head back on the dirt, stood, and looked up at the millions watching. The entire universe was silent before Him when He spoke.

"This man is My friend and a citizen of Heaven. Honor him."

After the Lord spoke, six other gladiators entered the arena: my friends Shawn, Sparky, Rob, Terry, my son-in-law Ben, and my son Chris. They picked me up and carried me back through the gates. Immediately I was transported to the heavenlies where I was very much alive. Now it was my turn to cheer on my friends who were fighting their own good fight of faith in the arena below.

Finally, my brethren, be strong in the Lord and in the power of His might. Put on the whole armor of God, that you may be able to stand against the wiles of the devil. For we do not wrestle against flesh and blood, but against principalities, against powers, against the rulers of the darkness of this age, against spiritual hosts of wickedness in the heavenly places.

EPHESIANS 6:10–12 (NKJV)

Being Honest with Myself:

Am I fighting the good fight of faith in order to win?

The Washer and Dryer

n the summer of 2000, my wife, Brenda, and I decided to remodel our house as well as add a room behind the kitchen. When I returned that September from a mission trip to El Salvador, we broke ground. With our friend, Ed, at the helm of the project, it moved along. Our hope was to have the project finished by Thanksgiving. As so many remodeling jobs go, Christmas came and went, and we still had not completed the job.

Now the fall and winter of 2000 in southwest Missouri were the coldest on record for many years. The back of our home behind the kitchen was torn off. Plastic sheeting was the only thing between the winter elements and us. The heater had been taken out; a new one was yet to be installed. The washer and dryer were unhooked because the tile had not yet been set in the laundry room.

So there we were: no stove and no washer and dryer. Our home was cold, even the refrigerator was in the uncarpeted living room, where we had also torn out the old fireplace. We resorted to eating out every day and going to the Laundromat almost every Saturday morning. It had been years since my wife and I had gone to the Laundromat (by the way, I think the same people who make slot machines make washers and dryers for Laundromats). We anxiously waited for the day when we could hook up our appliances again.

Several weeks came and went. The tile was almost completely laid in the laundry room. One day, my wife returned home and told me about something that had happened to our dear friend and neighbor. Her washer had gone out. She was a widow, and her funds were too tight to replace such a large appliance. We were standing in the kitchen as Brenda told me the story. I was staring at our washer and dryer, sitting in the corner, covered with plastic.

The Lord spoke to me at that moment: *"John, will you give her your washer and dryer?"*

Ours were not old, and both units worked fine. Brenda and I agreed. When our neighbor left to visit her daughter in North Carolina, she gave us the key to her house so my daughter, wife, and I could sleep in a warm house and take showers. With the key in hand, we removed her old washer and dryer and installed the new ones.

That would probably be a nice story in and of itself, except for the fact that this was more than just giving away two appliances. Several weeks later, when the remodeling was complete, we did not have the extra money to spend on a new washer and dryer for ourselves. Brenda and I were still visiting the Laundromat.

I remember saying, "Lord, I don't have the money for a new washer and dryer." I will never forget His response.

"John, I want you and Brenda to learn sacrifice through this. Anyone can give out of abundance, but not everyone will give out of sacrifice, and that is My heart."

I have not forgotten that lesson. For almost four more months, Brenda and I made the Saturday pilgrimage to laundry-land, until that blessed day came when we could purchase a new set for our home.

> *. . . It is more blessed to give than to receive . . .*
>
> ACTS 20:35 (NKJV)

Being Honest with Myself:

Is God showing me someone's need so I can help them and learn how to sacrifice?

Go by Bair's Grocery

had been in Branson all day working at the home of one of the Lennon sisters who lived on Lake Taneycomo. I had taken my Labrador, Aslan, with me; he loved the cold water of the lake. By evening, we were both ready to head home. I stopped by to say hi to my mother-in-law and then headed up Highway 65 back to Springfield. I had no sooner gotten out of Branson when the Lord spoke to me: *"John, I want you to go by Bair's Grocery."*

I knew right where that was because I filled up my truck there all the time. I did not need gas, but God had said to go. I put it out of my mind, turned on the radio, and headed north to the store. Bair's was out of my way, so I had to take a three-mile detour west to get over to the highway on which the store was located. I pulled in the station and thought I would top off my tank; that would save me a trip the next morning.

I walked into the store to buy a drink and pay for the fuel. As I stepped into the store, I noticed a man kind of hunkered down by an aisle I stayed away from: the pornography aisle. He turned slightly, and I immediately recognized him as the youth pastor of a local church. I heard God say, *"This is why I sent you here."*

I walked up behind him and put my arm around him; he turned quickly to see who it was. I called him by name and said, "I don't think Jesus wants you looking at X-rated porno, do you? In fact, I think He wants you to go back home to your wife and three kids."

You could have blown him over with a feather. He turned red, tears filled his eyes, and he walked outside. I got my drink and waited in line to pay. When I walked outside, my friend was standing in the parking lot, weeping. I walked over and put my arm around him. I asked him if he thought it might be time to get things right with God. He told me how his dad had been a deacon but read X-rated magazines his whole life. "I would sneak around and peek at them," he said. "I got hooked." I told my friend how God had told me to go by Bair's Grocery, and the reason was evident: God wanted him to get caught.

I did not see him for several months until I happened to walk by him in another grocery store. He came alongside me, put his hand on my shoulder, and said: "John, I'm free. Jesus set me free!" I was thrilled for him and told him so.

This is the only story I will write about things like this, but I have seen so many religious people, pastors, deacons, department heads, et cetera out with other men or women, being lured by lust into another's arms. Some I have confronted, and some I have not. I always walk away with a broken heart. Is it any wonder why we do not see revival or why we do not see God's power manifested in our churches and in our personal lives?

Psalm 51 records King David's confession to God about his sin. Let me encourage you: if you have any hidden sins, recognize that they are not really hidden. God sees every time you sneak around. God watches with a broken heart. Repent now—or He might send someone to expose you.

Create in me a clean heart, O God. Renew a loyal spirit within me.

PSALM 51:10 (NLT)

Being Honest with Myself:

Do I have sin I need to confess, sin I think is hidden?

Humiliated

do not know if you have ever had to speak to a crowd or not, but I think the worst thing that could happen would be for a speaker to get stage fright and freeze up. For years at three different churches I attended, I taught Sunday school. When I was in my twenties, it was the junior high kids. Then, after January 3, 1980, I taught an adult Sunday school class. Personally, I enjoy teaching adults.

When I was asked to teach a young adult class, I felt the Lord wanted me to accept the position. People in their mid-twenties made up the majority of the class. The Lord indicated that He wanted me to do this, so I jumped in with both feet. Things were going well. I studied hard so I could hear God and tell the class what I thought He wanted to say. This is something I am adamant about, as I believe anyone who teaches or preaches should be anointed and have a fresh word from God.

One particular week, as I was preparing for the lesson, the Lord spoke to me:

"John, talk about friends this week."

I said okay and then spent the whole week studying friends and friendship, anything related to the subject. I felt adequately prepared for the lesson and went into the Sunday school class confident that I had something to say that was from the Lord. The class was full that week, and there was not much room left for people to sit down. When all the class announcements and preliminaries were over, I stood to speak. But God had something different in mind that day.

Even though I had studied, I could not think of anything to say. My mind went blank as God's anointing left me. I tried to get started but could not. Then I thought I would "wing it." I could not do that either. I was not getting anywhere, so after about ten minutes, I told the class that there was no anointing on me to speak. Embarrassed, I walked over to an open seat and sat down. Right then, the Lord spoke these words to me:

"John, I am the vine and you are the branches—without me, you can do nothing."

John 15:5; a familiar verse.

Why such a simple story? Because today, years later, it is still true. Without Him, I can do nothing. Without Him, *you* can do nothing—nothing of eternal value, nothing that makes it through the fire when God tries our works to see if they are gold, silver, precious stone, or wood, hay and stubble.

A very simple story, yes, but one with a profound message. God wants you to know that without Him at the helm, without Him guiding your life, you will do nothing of eternal value.

> *For I have been crucified with Christ, nevertheless I live; yet not I, but Christ liveth in me: and the life which I now live in the flesh I live by the faith of the Son of God, who loved me, and gave himself for me.*
>
> GALATIANS 2:20 (KJV)

Being Honest with Myself:

Have I been humiliated trying to live the Christian life?
Have I realized that God wants to show me that without Him, I can do nothing?

The Angry Jew

n 1995 my wife Brenda was managing her mother's gift shop in Branson, Missouri. Managing a gift shop requires trips to markets around the country to view the new products available for your store. The gift market in Dallas, Texas, took place in January that year.

The landscaping business comes to a complete halt around that time of year, so I thought I would go to Dallas with Brenda. I had never been to a gift market, and I wasn't quite prepared for the enormity of the place. I could not believe how huge it was, how much stuff there was. I do not think it would be an exaggeration to say there were millions of items.

It did not take long for me to realize I had a problem. My mother-in-law, wife, and the others in the group planned on looking at every item. I realized something that day: shopping is not my thing. I quickly found myself wandering off to keep from getting bored.

A big part of the market was dedicated to jewelry. About lunchtime, I found myself wandering from store to store, looking for the best free food being offered. I drifted in and out of jewelry stores, eating hors d'oeuvres. I was standing by an appetizer table when a young Jewish fellow walked in, a briefcase handcuffed to his wrist. He walked straight up to the food table and started picking through the finger food. Since I never met a stranger, I started a conversation with him.

"Where are you from?" I asked.

"Israel," he replied.

"Really? I've always wanted to visit Israel."

"Yeah. You should do that."

"Well," I said. "I've always wanted to visit the places where Jesus lived and died."

At that comment, this young Jewish fellow's countenance changed immediately. He became vehement, moved so his face was within six inches of mine, and began to yell.

"I'll bet you think we are Christ-killers, don't you?" he screamed. "I'll bet you think His blood is on our hands, don't you?" The yelling was getting louder and louder, and people were beginning to stare. "I'll bet you think it's all our fault, don't you?"

To tell you the truth, I do not normally do well with people in my face, but the Lord intervened: *"John, keep your cool."*

This young man finally said all he had to say and began to cool down. It was then that Jesus spoke to me and gave me the words to convey to this young man. I relayed what I felt like the Lord wanted me to say:

"Actually, I want to thank you for how much the Jewish people mean to me. If it weren't for the Jews, I wouldn't be saved. I wouldn't have the Bible, both Old and New Testaments. And no, I don't personally blame the Jews, for Jesus said God so loved the world that He gave His only begotten Son, that whosoever believes in Him should not perish but have everlasting life. And while it's true that both Jews and Romans killed Him, my sin put Him there, also."

When I had told him that, I paused and then continued. "John 10:18 says, 'No one takes my life from me, but I lay it down of myself. I have power to lay it down, and I have power to take it up again. This command I have received from my Father.' So no, you're not Christ-killers; Jesus died of his own accord. For you and for me. Period."

The young Jewish fellow did not say a word, he just walked away.

I wish I could tell you that young Hebrew repented or at least said, "Well, I will study this issue, think on it, pray on it." But I cannot tell you any more about him other than a seed was planted that hopefully took root.

When the movie *The Passion of Christ* came out, some misinformed people labeled Christians as anti-Semitic. Comments or beliefs from people in the past have fueled confusion on this subject, and many Jews have subsequently felt rejection by the Christian community that is not there—or should not be there. Let me clear up this confusion with the truth: I can tell you who killed Jesus, who bears the responsibility for His blood. It was me; it was you; it was the world. He died for all our sins, and He did it so *all of us* could have a relationship with Him.

What about you? Has it ever sunk in that Jesus—who is GOD—left Heaven for you, suffered for you, died for you? And that this Jesus loves you just the way you are, no matter who you are, what background you came from, or how many rotten things you have done? Why not commit your life to the King who became poor that you might become rich? And if you have done that, but you have wandered off, why not come back to the lover of your soul?

> *But God demonstrates His own love toward us, in that while we were still sinners, Christ died for us.*
>
> ROMANS 5:8 (NKJV)

> *There is neither Jew nor Greek, slave nor free, male nor female, for you are all one in Christ Jesus.*
>
> GALATIANS 3:28 (NIV)

Being Honest with Myself:

Do I honestly look for opportunities to share my faith, the good news, with others?

Chicken and Catfish

We had made our way to Venezuela into a remote village in the Amazon region called Atabapo. The village sits on a peninsula between two rivers. It is a simple trading post destination for native Indians. About 1,500 soldiers protect the people from the Columbian guerillas located just on the other side of the river. The guerillas wreak havoc whenever they can. Eight of us from three different states in America had gone to build a home for the missionary serving that area, whose name was Bob.

Our job was to lay block for the exterior and interior walls as well as a cellar. The blocks were handmade onsite out of materials brought two hundred miles down river. Although the heat was stifling (the temperature reached 110 degrees with extremely high humidity during the day and no lower than eighty degrees at night), our work went well; the house was built in record time.

Most evenings we would sit around under the palm branch arbor, laughing and kidding around while lying on hammocks. Since we were outsiders, people would stop by to see the Americans who had come to work on the home. People who attended the church would come by to pay their respects, too. One particular night, we had finished eating, and most of us had taken our showers at the water tower just down the street. We were sitting around shooting the breeze when a man came walking up from behind the house carrying a bowl of catfish and a chicken. He presented his chicken and the bowl full of catfish to the pastor. The man who brought the gifts was smiling from ear to ear. I saw that a third of his teeth were missing, but he was happy. It was obvious that whatever he was doing made him feel good. We offered him a drink and some food, which he gladly accepted. Since most of us there didn't speak Spanish, we were very curious as to what had just occurred.

Bob explained that this was a simple native who lived somewhere up the river. He had come down to Atabapo to bring his tithe: a bowl of baby catfish and a chicken. I looked around as Bob interpreted the event we were participating in and noticed there was not a dry eye in the place. The Lord spoke volumes to everyone through that man. To me, the Lord said this: *"John, never forget what you have witnessed here tonight. It is more blessed to give than to receive; that is why he has that smile."*

The truth is that God can do more with 90 percent than you can with 100 percent. I heard Larry Burkett on the radio once say that Christians on average give only 2–3 percent as their tithes. Just think what we could do if we simply believed God.

> *"Will a man rob God? Yet you rob me. But you ask, 'how do we rob you?' In tithes and offerings. You are under a curse—the whole nation of you—because you are robbing me. Bring the whole tithe into the storehouse, that there may be food in my house. Test me in this," says the Lord Almighty, "and see if I will not throw open the floodgates of heaven and pour out so much blessing that you will not have room enough for it."*
>
> MALACHI 3:8–10 (NIV)

Being Honest with Myself:

Have I been robbing God of the 10 percent tithe I owe Him? Do I need to trust in His promise that He will provide?

Any Minute

Most of my life, I do not remember feeling well. From the time I was very young, I was always tired. Once in a while I would feel all right for a day, but that eating-too-much-sugar-and-then-crashing feeling was the one that dominated most of my days. In my teen years through my 20s, I would sleep ten to twelve hours a day and still feel tired.

As I approached my late 30s, I started feeling death in myself. That is difficult to describe, but nonetheless, I had a strong inner sense that I was dying. Numerous visits to different doctors turned up only one thing: I had extremely high blood pressure. Most of the time, my blood pressure was between 180–210 over 120–140—and this was the low end of my readings. Besides being tired, I was depressed most of the time. The pressure in my head made it feel like it was going to explode. This was a regular occurrence and made me want to sleep even more.

By my late 30s I found myself sleeping 12–15 hours a day. This was very frustrating for me because this was a time when most men pursue their careers with vigor. As you can imagine, my wife became very frustrated, although she handled it as well as could be expected. To top it all off, when the pressure got so great in my head, I would blow up emotionally. I could not stand it. Many times I would go somewhere alone and beat my head with the palm of my hand, desperate for the pressure to go away. As a Christian, I felt tremendous guilt over this. In spite of that guilt, I still got up and prayed every morning. I lived an odd life.

Then, on top of 15 hours a day of sleep, depression, and blowing my stack, I began to get major nose bleeds. By the fall of 1993, I had deteriorated to the point that I could barely work and felt miserable 24 hours a day. One day, the Lord spoke to me and told me to take my family on a vacation. I picked Disney World in Florida. We left the day after Thanksgiving for a week. I felt good every day that week for the first time in my whole life—and I was 41 years old. The feeling was so abnormal that it is still vivid to this day.

But when we returned home from vacation, a downward spiral began. I could barely put one foot in front of the other. I knew death was eminent, but I did not say much. I thought people would think I was crazy since I could not point to anything specific. That was when the Lord intervened. While He never said a word to me, He orchestrated the circumstances to save my life.

The landscape business in Missouri is typically a March through November business, so any work one would get in mid-December is unusual unless it is snow plowing. But that December, I got a call from a doctor's wife who wanted two trees planted in her backyard before Christmas. She said her parents were coming for the holidays, and she wanted the trees in the yard. I tried to talk her out of it, but she was insistent. I purchased the two maples and hired a day laborer to help dig the holes. I will never forget being so exhausted from taking the two large maples to Dr. Buckner's backyard. I sat down on one of the tree balls to rest.

When I looked up, the doctor was coming toward me. I stood up to greet him. He walked up to me and the first words out his mouth were: "John, I like the trees, but you don't look so good." I simply told him I did not feel good, and I was going home to go to bed as soon as the trees were planted.

"John," Dr. Buckner said. "I want you to go see an internist friend of mine, Dr. Evans. I'll make sure you get in."

I told him that I had not felt well for a long time, and that it was probably my high blood pressure. He pushed the issue again, so I promised him I would think about it and give his friend a call.

The trees were finally planted, and I went home to bed. The next day I told Brenda about Dr. Buckner's suggestion. She thought it was a good idea. The appointment was set for January, 1994.

Dr. Evans was a very pleasant man with a good bedside manner. "John," he said. "Hop up here on the table; the nurse is going to take your blood pressure."

I made the comment that it would be high. He left the room, and the nurse took my blood pressure. Dr. Evans returned, saying, "Your blood pressure is pretty high for someone no larger than you are." Then he asked me an odd question. "John, has anyone ever taken the blood pressure in your feet?"

They had not. "No, sir," I replied. The nurse put the cuff around my ankle. After two attempts to get a pressure reading, the nurse looked bewildered. She rolled her eyes toward the doctor.

"I can't get it, Dr. Evans," she said. They left the room together to get a machine called a *Dinamap* that is able to take sensitive readings. He took the reading in my ankles, looked at the machine, and walked out of the room with a muddled look on his face. He never said a word to me. Fifteen minutes later, he returned, pulled up a stool, and sat there in front of me.

"John," he said finally, "if you have what I think you have, I don't know how you are alive." He shook his head and continued. "In fact, it is impossible for you to be alive if you have what I think you have."

"What's wrong with me?" I interrupted.

"I can't be sure without an angiogram," he said, "but I think you have what is called a coarctation of the aorta." Without explaining to me what that was, he simply stated a second time that he did not know how I was alive. Mixed emotions rushed through me as he continued. "Here is what you are going to do: go home, sit down, and do nothing. I don't want you doing even menial chores until I can get a radiologist to check you out. You could die any minute." He paused. "I will call you when we are ready for you. John, I just don't know how to say this gently: I don't know how you are living. You could die any minute."

I drove the half mile home. I remember my wife was cooking dinner.

"The doctor says I'm dying," I told her. We wept in each others arms. Within thirty minutes, the phone rang. My mother-in-law was on the line, and she sounded upset.

"What's wrong with John?" she cried. "The Lord has put him strong on my heart."

My wife did not know much more than what she told her mother: "He's dying." I did not even know how to say "coarctation of the aorta." I sat down, ate a little, and went to bed as usual. I was exhausted.

Before I fell asleep, it truly hit me, and tears flooded my eyes. Any minute I could die. Any minute it could be over. I was going to have to face God—was I ready? What would I say? My thoughts raced toward my wife, children, and friends. "Any minute," the doctor had said, over and over. I fell asleep thinking "any minute!"

> . . . *It is appointed for men to die once and after this comes judgment . . .*
>
> HEBREWS 9:27 (NAS)

Being Honest with Myself:

Am I ready for eternity? Do I realize my time could come at any minute?

Trust Me

When people are told they could die any minute, they have one of two mindsets: first, panic, fear, and apprehension; second: trust in God while waiting. By grace I chose the latter. There was a week and a half of wait-time between being told I was dying and receiving an angiogram. Dr. Evans had wanted a particular physician to do the work, so we were waiting until he returned from vacation.

During this time, my in-laws had sold their home. So my kids pitched in to help pack. Everyone was dogmatic; I sat around and watched.

I have always found it humorous how God speaks to us in unusual places. While I was in the restroom one day that week washing my hands, a piece of paper from behind the mirror floated like a maple seed down to the floor. I did not think too much about it, but I thought I would pick it up and throw it away. When I glanced down at it, I saw Psalm 91:15 (NIV):

> He shall call upon me, and I will answer him. I will be with him in trouble, I will deliver him and honor him.

I read that verse two or three times; it impacted me immensely. The great "I AM" had spoken. I still carry that verse in my wallet, even today. How that little piece of paper got behind that mirror, and how it was blown to the floor at just the right time, well . . . what do you think? God used it to encourage me at one of my hardest times.

Not many days afterward, I got the call to report to the hospital for the angiogram. This was not anything I was looking forward to;

the procedure includes cutting a person in the groin area, inserting a tube into the main artery, then feeding the tube up through the artery until it reaches your heart. There is a camera of sorts where the medical staff can see what is going on inside the heart on monitors. You are not knocked out, but you are in a stupor from the drugs. If you want, you can watch the same monitors the staff sees.

I was rolled down from my room to radiology, the doc made his cut, and the tube started north. Out of the clear blue, the doctor said, "Wait! I'm going to change and do this guy through the armpit instead." He mentioned that he did not do more than one in a hundred people that way. They pulled the tube back out, cut my armpit, and away we went. I lay there and thought, *Great. Two cuts for the price of one.*

As Dr. Evans had suspected, I had a coarctation of the aorta, a severe kink in the aorta. My aorta was about the size of a pencil lead; a normal aorta is about the size of a fifty-cent piece. Had they proceeded with the tube from my groin area to the heart, they would have ruptured the aorta and I would have died. Question: Who made the doctor change his mind midstream?

I remember two more things from that day; one: the doctor saying "I don't believe this," and two: the staff wanting to know how I had two kids. I will let you figure out that riddle. I was finally taken upstairs to a room in which I spent the night. Dr. Evans came in and said my x-ray was "X-Ray of the Year" around there and was the talk of the medical community. I keep a copy of it in my office as a reminder of who holds my life in His hands.

The next morning, I made the comment to Dr. Evans that the Catholic hospital in town was known for their heart department. He looked at me strangely and said, "John, you don't understand. We are trying to find someone anywhere who has operated on someone like you! You will have to go away for the surgery." He continued, "We've talked to Duke, Phoenix Heart Institute, and Johns Hopkins to name a few, and no one has seen anyone your age with this problem."

My friend Andy has a brother who is a financial dean at Harvard. He checked there, and again, no one had ever seen anyone my age alive with a coarctation of the aorta. I am not quite sure who found the information, but we learned that Barnes Hospital in St. Louis had operated on a man with the same defect. He was 21 years old. I was 41. We decided to go.

The time from the angiogram to the heart surgery was about three weeks. During those three weeks were three Sundays. Each Sunday I would walk down the aisle to have the elders pray that God would heal me so I would not have to go through the surgery.

The first two Sundays, God never said a word. For two weeks, God was completely silent. On the third Sunday, when I walked down to be prayed for, He finally spoke when I was on my way back to my seat. This is what He said:

"John, I'm not going to heal you. You are going through the surgery, and I am not going to tell you how it is going to turn out. I am going to ask you to trust Me."

Now, let me ask you, do you trust God? Before you jump on the answer, think it through. *Do you trust God?* For your bad marriage, your runaway child, your business, your medical problem? Do you trust God with your very life? Or do you trust yourself, your money, your position, or your savvy?

Live or die, my life was in His hands. But isn't it, anyway?

My times are in Your hand . . .

PSALM 31:15 (NKJV)

Oh, taste and see that the Lord is good; blessed is the man who trusts in Him!

PSALM 34:8 (NKJV)

Being Honest with Myself:

Do I trust God with everything—even my life?

Heart Surgery and Beyond

My friend Sparky and my wife Brenda took me to Barnes Hospital in St. Louis. I sat in the back of the van and slept most of the way there. Our appointment there was with the chief of surgery. Also meeting us was the head of surgery for the children's hospital in St. Louis, Dr. Huddleston. Dr. Huddleston is a thoracic pediatric surgeon. After reviewing the x-rays from Springfield, both doctors confirmed that I had been born with a severe coarctation of the aorta.

At this point, Dr. Huddleston took me aside to tell me what he thought the odds were and what complications might occur. He gave me an overview of the procedure, which he anticipated would take six to eight hours. I remember him telling me about the problems that could occur, since he would be operating on my aorta, which is next to my spinal cord. The longer he was in that area, the greater the chances for complications. None of these complications were any more appealing than having your fingernails pulled out with pliers.

We walked back into the room where my wife and friend were waiting. They asked, "When do you want to do the surgery?" The doctors all agreed it needed to happen immediately, citing the fact that they believed I would not make it much longer. When I heard them say "in the morning," all I kept thinking was *"drive-through heart surgery."* I told the doctors I was not quite ready to go through it that soon. I told them that God had somehow kept me alive for 41 years, and He could keep me alive for one more week. I told them I would be back in exactly one week. In the back of my mind, I just wanted to have a week to sit before the Lord and "tidy up" some things.

We drove home, and I began a week of contemplating what it would be like to die. Mind you, it was not a morbid thing, but I had to accept the fact that I could die or become a vegetable. I believe that week was one of the nicest I have ever had with the Lord. He was not necessarily saying anything profound to me; I think it was more the peace that I felt. I spent the week making sure there was not anything I would be ashamed of when I got to Heaven. I had a lawyer make me a living will in case I was to end up looking like Trog the alien. I did not want that. I told my wife to make sure to "trip" over the power cord if they said I would have to exist on tubes. The week went by very quickly, and I was off to the Gateway city to find my fate.

For the next day or two, I was put through every conceivable test. I felt like a blood bank. Then yet another angiogram was performed, another of this, another of that. I signed papers giving the hospital the right to film my operation. Barnes is a teaching hospital, so my operation took place in an auditorium-type room. Countless students, doctors, and nurses interviewed me. The morning came, and I said my goodbyes to family and friends.

I told my wife that I did not want anyone to be sued if things did not go well or if I died; it was no one's fault I was born with a severe heart defect. Dr. Huddleston informed me that due to that defect, my heart was the age of a 65 or 70-year-old man's. I figured these people would do the best they could. No matter the outcome, I knew I was in God's hands. That is the last thing I remember thinking.

Thirty-six hours later, I woke up in my hospital room.

I returned home on my daughter's birthday, February 17, 1994, with strict orders to not do anything for three to four months. I could not even lift a gallon of milk. The first ten days were horrible; I could not sleep for more than twenty minutes a day. The three months passed slowly, but God brought me through. I had lots of time to spend with Jehovah Rapha.

Today as I sit here, looking out the window and writing this story, I am reminded that ten years ago today I was literally in God's hands. I am still in God's hands today, and so are you. Although I have not mentioned it to Him in quite some time, He has not yet provided me with answers on one thing I always wonder about: while so many other people were doing wonderful things with their lives, I was basically sleeping mine away for 41 years. Now I just figure that if that is part of what it took for Him to be glorified, then I am fine with it. He has the right to do as He pleases.

He is God, after all.

> . . . For in Him we live and move and have our being, as also some of your own poets have said, 'For we are also His offspring.'
>
> ACTS 17:28 (NKJV)

> And we know that all things work together for good to those who love God, to those who are the called according to His purpose.
>
> ROMANS 8:28 (NKJV)

Being Honest with Myself:

When things don't always go the way I would like them to, do I still believe God is faithful?

You know what? God is out to glorify Himself on earth . . . and He just might use you.

Your Story

Do I Need to Make a Commitment to Christ?

> *"Enter through the narrow gate. For wide is the gate and broad is the road that leads to destruction, and many enter through it. But small is the gate and narrow the road that leads to life, and only a few find it." Matthew 7:13–14 (NIV).*

Jeremiah 17:9 says the human heart is "deceitful above all things and beyond cure" (NIV). Ezekiel 11:19 states that God can remove a deceitful heart and replace it with a heart of "flesh" and that the result will be a supernatural ability to live a God-focused life.

We begin our journey with Christ by becoming like little children, approaching Him in meekness and humility (Matthew 18:3). "There is not a righteous man on earth who does what is right and never sins" (Ecclesiastes 7:20, NIV); we must admit our inability to change our own pattern of sin or wash away our own guilt.

> *. . . for all have sinned and fall short of the glory of God, and are justified freely by his grace through the redemption that came by Christ Jesus. God presented him as a sacrifice of atonement through faith in his blood. He did this to demonstrate his justice, because in his forbearance he had left the sins committed beforehand unpunished—he did it to demonstrate his justice at the present time, so as to be just and the one who justifies those who have faith in Jesus (Romans 3:23–26 NIV).*

Hebrews 10:3–4 explains the purpose of the animal sacrifices God required before Christ came: "But those sacrifices are an annual reminder of sins, because it is impossible for the blood of bulls and goats to take away sins" (NIV). However, Hebrews 9:22 (NIV) reminds us that "without the shedding of blood, there is no forgiveness." The reconciliation of this was Jesus. He lived a sinless life and gave up that life as a "ransom" for many (Matthew 20:28). At the cross, God supernaturally placed every sin believers would ever commit on Jesus (perfect, spotless, sinless Jesus) and punished Him for them (Romans 3:24–25).

When we wholeheartedly put our faith in Jesus, in His sacrificial atonement for our sin, God covers our sinful life—every terrible action or thought, whether vicious murder or childish selfishness— with Jesus' perfect, sinless life so we can walk with God today and live with Him forever when we die. Hebrews 11:6 says that "without faith, it is impossible to please God" (NIV). But when we have this faith, we have blessed assurance for the future, and peace and God's guidance for today.

Am I Following Christ with Passion, or Do I Need to Repent of Leaving My First Love?

> . . . let us throw off everything that hinders and the sin that so
> easily entangles, and let us run with perseverance the race marked
> out for us. Let us fix our eyes on Jesus . . . Hebrews 12:1–2 (NIV).

Our view of God has a direct impact on our faith: if we view Him as uninterested, our faith will reflect that and be less than if we see Him as intimately involved in our lives. A manifestation of "lesser" faith is a lack of submission to the Lord and His commands. Jesus said, "If anyone loves me, he will obey my teaching . . . He who does not love me will not obey my teaching" (John 14:23–24, NIV). However, God realizes that through our own power, we could never live the Christian life—but He has promised to live through us so we can have victory over sin. 2 Peter 1:3–11 says:

> His divine power has given us everything we need for life and
> godliness through our knowledge of him who called us by his own
> glory and goodness. Through these he has given us his very great
> and precious promises, so that through them you may participate
> in the divine nature and escape the corruption in the world
> caused by evil desires. For this very reason, make every effort to

add to your faith goodness; and to goodness, knowledge; and to knowledge, self-control; and to self-control, perseverance; and to perseverance, godliness; and to godliness, brotherly kindness; and to brotherly kindness, love. For if you possess these qualities in increasing measure, they will keep you from being ineffective and unproductive in your knowledge of our Lord Jesus Christ. But if anyone does not have them, he is nearsighted and blind, and has forgotten that he has been cleansed from his past sins. Therefore, my brothers, be all the more eager to make your calling and election sure. For if you do these things, you will never fall, and you will receive a rich welcome into the eternal kingdom of our Lord and Savior Jesus Christ.

The world will always present options that will compromise our moral purity. Guard against such corruption that entangles. If God is stirring your heart that has been cold toward Him, repent and come back to Him quickly! He loves you with an everlasting love (Jeremiah 31:3).

To Be Continued . . .

TATE PUBLISHING & *Enterprises*

Tate Publishing is committed to excellence in the publishing industry. Our staff of highly trained professionals, including editors, graphic designers, and marketing personnel, work together to produce the very finest books available. The company reflects the philosophy established by the founders, based on Psalms 68:11,

"THE LORD GAVE THE WORD AND GREAT WAS THE COMPANY OF THOSE WHO PUBLISHED IT."

If you would like further information, please call
1.888.361.9473
or visit our website
www.tatepublishing.com

TATE PUBLISHING & *Enterprises*, LLC
127 E. Trade Center Terrace
Mustang, Oklahoma 73064 USA